LESS TOXIC LIVING

GREEN GABLES PRESS

LESS TOXIC LIVING

HOW TO REDUCE YOUR EVERYDAY EXPOSURE
TO TOXIC CHEMICALS:
AN INTRODUCTION FOR FAMILIES

KIRSTEN MCCULLOCH

GREEN GABLES PRESS
CANBERRA

Edited by Kirsten McCulloch
Proofreaders Leonie McCulloch & Christopher Howe
Cover design by Green Gables Design

Green Gables Press
PO Box 2026
Canberra, ACT 2902
www.greengablespress.com

Book Layout ©2013 BookDesignTemplates.com

Ordering Information:
Quantity sales. Special discounts are available on quantity purchases by corporations, associations, and others. For details, contact the 'Special Sales Department' at the address above.

Less Toxic Living: How to Reduce Your Everyday Exposure to
Toxic Chemicals—an Introduction for Families/
Kirsten McCulloch. —1st ed.
ISBN 978-0-9923699-0-3

Many, many thanks to my lovely family:
my husband Chris, and my children Liam, Mikaela and Eliane,
whose support, patience and willingness to test recipes and
techniques has made this book possible.

This book is for them and for every family or individual who wants
to live a life less toxic for themselves and for the planet.

CONTENTS

ACKNOWLEDGEMENTS

Many, many thanks to all the contributors of this book. Not only have they either written new material or graciously allowed me to reproduce their work here for your benefit, but many of them consistently research, test and write about living a more sustainable, less toxic life, simply in the hope that their experience might help someone else.

Thanks also go to all my wonderful beta readers, who read and proofread early copies, providing me with such excellent feedback. There are too many of you to name, but I would like to give special thanks to my mother, Leonie McCulloch, who has always been my greatest proofreader and a huge support.

And finally, my heartfelt thanks go to my wonderful husband Chris, who has always supported me as a writer, even when on occasion—and especially for the production of this book—it's taken up my weekends and evenings (as well as days), leaving him doing the largest part of the kid wrangling and house work.

COPYRIGHT ACKNOWLEDGEMENTS

Many thanks to authors and publishers for permission to reproduce the following. Articles not listed here are original work and copyright remains with the individual authors.

Page 13 'Clear the Air With Indoor Plants' ©2013 Tricia Hogbin, first published in the Newcastle Herald, 16 July 2013, republished with permission of the author.

Page 145 'Is BPS the New Mystery Chemical in BPA-free Plastic Food Containers and Cans?' ©2013 Alicia Voorhies. A previous version of this article appeared on http://guide.thesoftlanding.com.

Page 149 'What's in Our Products: A Brief Look at Parabens' ©2013 Melissa Goodwin, a previous version of this article appeared in 2010 on http://frugalandthriving.com.au.

Page 161 'Nanos and Sunscreen: Are Shade, Shirts and Hats the Safer Option?' ©2013 Kate Hennessy. This story first appeared on http://parenting.kidspot.com.au without the 'Note'. Republished with permission of Kidspot.

Page 169 'Homemade Probiotic Deodorant—That Really Works!' ©2011 Andrea Muse, http://frugallysustainable.com.

Page 175 'Forty Second Home Made Body Scrub' ©2013 Alexx Stuart, http://alexxstuart.com.

Page 177 'Is Your Lip Balm Drying You Out? Here's How to Make Your Own' ©2013 Kirsten McCulloch, a previous version of this article was published on http://safecosmeticsaustralia.com.au.

GETTING STARTED

KATHY, AN AUSTRALIAN mother of three, cut most food additives out of her family's diet in an attempt to get her four year old's behaviour and asthma under control.[1]

'Mirrim had an asthma attack when we were driving home one day,' she told me. 'We were about 20 minutes from home when it started, and the ventolin just wasn't helping. It was really terrifying. Luckily we were passing near my husband's work, so we pulled in there and called an ambulance.'

It wasn't the first time an ambulance had been needed to get Mirrim's breathing under control, but perhaps it will be the last. She hasn't had an attack since the family's change in diet, though the warmer weather may also have made a difference. It isn't only the asthma that's improved though.

'She would go into these massive rages,' Kathy said, 'and I could see in her eyes she didn't know what was happening, or how to stop it.' The rages, as well as the asthma, have stopped along with the food additives. 'She still has normal kid tantrums, but it's not the same,' Kathy said.

---

[1] Names have been changed to protect privacy.

IN THE PAST hundred years and more there have been many marvellous discoveries made, which have arguably made life easier for many people and have certainly saved lives.

However, in that time, there have also been some terrible discoveries made, and along with them, some terrible decisions. Among them was the decision to put economic growth ahead of our health, and the health of the planet. In so doing we have not only allowed thousands of chemicals, seventy-five per cent of them untested for safety, to fill our homes, soil and waterways,[2] we have also lost numerous old skills that our grandparents took for granted.

Few of us now have skills of building, repairing, growing our own food, and yes, making our own cleaning and personal care products. We've also lost the skills of making do with what we have or can easily grow.

It's not only that we've lost skills, there are also skills we've never developed effectively, that we need in order to live well in such a toxic world. Skills such as label reading and asking questions.

We naturally assume, don't we, that our governments, having our best interests at heart, would ensure that the chemicals added to our foods and skincare products, furniture and domestic cleaning products are safe.

Sadly, that just isn't true. In the pages of this book you will read that seventy-five per cent of the chemicals registered for use in Australia have never been tested for human or environmental safety; that of 2983 fragrance chemicals

---

[2] See chapter 8 What is Really Lurking Under Your Sink?

evaluated by the US National Institute of Occupational Health and Safety, 884 were found to be toxic.

Is it that the government really doesn't care about us at all? No, it's not that simple. Rather, there are always competing interests at work: honest economic interests, including the desire of governments for economic growth rather than recession, as well as the interests of industry lobbyists and politicians who want to get re-elected (for good reasons as well as bad).

Does that make it okay that we have these toxic chemicals in our homes and waterways and in our very bodies? Not at all. Things need to change. One way to be part of that is to educate ourselves, and then vote with our dollars. Stop supporting companies that pollute and poison us and our children and our planet. Stop accepting that we have to have those toxins in our homes.

This book is intended as an introduction to various aspects of toxic and less toxic living, including some practical solutions. I don't call it non-toxic living, because when you are born today, you already have toxic chemicals circulating in your body, from brominated fire retardants to pesticides, from artificial musks to chemicals used in plastics.[3]

But we can reduce our ongoing exposure to chemicals, by making some relatively simple changes, as well as some more complex ones. This book covers some of each, and is intended as a way for you to get started, or continue on your journey to make changes, without being overwhelming.

---

[3] Sarah Lantz, *Chemical Free Kids*, 2nd Edition, 2012, pp 47-48.

JONATHON WILSON FULLER, made famous by
the movie *The Boy in the Plastic Bubble*, is considered to be
one of the most chemically sensitive people in the world.
Jonathon is sensitive to food additives and VOCs (volatile
organic compounds) including perfumes, pesticides and
industrial chemicals. The TV movie showed him as a 17-
year-old boy, breathing purified air, and unable to leave his
own home. His father worked in industrial chemistry for
many years, until he realised that when he was on holidays
his son's health improved, only to worsen again when he
returned to work and came home with industrial chemicals
leaking into the air from his breath and skin.[4]

Clearly most people are not as sensitive to chemicals as
Jonathon. For many of us, an obvious chemical sensitivity
will never develop. But in some cases the cancer we get
down the track may be related to the carcinogenic compounds in our daily moisturiser or cleaning products. And
the evidence of many individuals' stories is that most people don't realise the effects chemicals are having on them,
until they get markedly worse.

In her book, *Chemical Free Kids*, Dr Sarah Lantz relates
the story of Leena, a hairdresser who started getting particularly bad eczema and dermatitis about 10 years into her ca-
reer. Another year on, she started getting aches and pains,
swollen joints, bleeding gums and migraines. 'I knew the
dermatitis was probably due to my profession, but I didn't

---

[4] See Sue Dengate *Fed Up: Understanding how food affects your child and
what you can do about it*, Random House Australia, North Sydney, 2008,
pp. 154-155.

think the other symptoms were related to my job as well,' she said.[5]

As it turned out, all the symptoms were related to the toxic burden her body was carrying, perhaps not only due to her own profession, but due to its impact on top of having grown up with a mother who was also a hairdresser. It took seeking help for her extremely colicky baby, Mia, following a difficult pregnancy and early birth, for Leena to get her own symptoms under control. Eventually, with the help of a nurse, a dietitian and a naturopath, she changed her diet, changed most of her cleaning products, and got rid of all her cosmetics, hair products, and anything with perfumes. Eventually she was able to go back to work in a chemical-free salon. Not surprisingly, as Leena's health got better, so did Mia's.

I hope that you are reading this book not because you, or your children, have significantly bad symptoms of chemical sensitivity, but because you know that the chemicals in our lives can affect us in ways we are unaware of until later. Whatever your reasons, I believe you will find some real solutions in this book, some ways to reduce your daily chemical exposure, and plenty of ideas for where to go next.

Kirsten McCulloch

---

[5] Lantz, *Chemical Free Kids*, p. 109.

How to Use This Book

LESS TOXIC LIVING can be useful whether you are just beginning to reduce your toxin exposure or you have been making changes for a while. The intention is to inspire you to think about things a little differently, to give you practical strategies for change and to prompt further research in areas that concern you.

You don't need to read the book all the way through or in any particular order. Since the intention is to give you a variety of practical starting points for moving to less toxic living, you can begin with any section of the book. Choose the area that most appeals to you, or that you have yet to look at.

I suggest reading one theoretical chapter and one practical or 'how to' chapter (some are both), and then picking one practical change to make first. Many of the articles also have references for further reading.

Some of the chapters in this book have appeared before, sometimes in a slightly different form, in magazines or on the authors' blogs. Consequently there are a wide variety of styles, and some chapters are short 'how-to' articles, while others are more in depth or theoretical. Some are based on the writer's individual experience and others are specifically research and science based. In some areas, the science simply isn't complete enough yet to make a decisive statement 'this is toxic' or 'that's harmless.' In those areas, I prefer to practice the precautionary principle, and try to reduce my exposure in sensible ways.

Each chapter begins with a short 'author bio' to give you an understanding of their backgrounds. For more detail about the contributors, and how you can connect with them on social media, see 'About the Contributors' at the end of the book. There is also more information about each contributor on the website: http://lesstoxicliving.net.

Accompanying this book are some free bonus downloads on the website, including printables and more. These special extras are only available after you purchase a copy of the book, so check out your special access code in the back of the book (just before the index).

A final editor's note:

As many of the articles have been published previously, their assumed audiences differ. Specifically, some are Australian while others are American. The situations in these two countries are similar enough that all articles will be relevant to at least these two audiences, though there are some minor differences in approved chemicals.

I have standardised punctuation through the book to use Australian conventions, but I have left original spelling, whether US or Australian English.

YOUR HOME

There are many small changes you can make in your home to reduce toxin exposure. Some of them are covered in other sections of this book, each of which looks at a specific area of your life or home. This section covers some more general changes you can make in your home, from growing house plants to getting rid of 'air fresheners' to some simple ways to detoxify your medicine cabinet.

[1]

Clear the Air With Indoor Plants

TRICIA HOGBIN

Tricia Hogbin is a project manager for The Australian Network for Plant Conservation. She is also an Australian writer and mother, who writes about learning to live better with less. She writes a regular column for the Newcastle Herald called 'Less is More', and blogs at Little Eco Footprints: *http://www.littleecofootprints.com*

AIR POLLUTION INSIDE our homes can be worse than the pollution found outside. As most of us spend a lot of time indoors, improving indoor air quality is worth considering. Thankfully, all it takes is a few indoor plants to clear the air.[6]

Our homes can be polluted with a mixture of volatile organic compounds (VOCs) that are emitted as vapour from

---

[6] Fraser Torpy 'Clearing the air: the hidden wonders of indoor plants' *The Conversation* http://theconversation.com/clearing-the-air-the-hidden-wonders-of-indoor-plants-15339

plastics, cleaning products, carpets, paint, cosmetics, and electronic equipment. Gas cookers and unflued gas heaters can also elevate carbon dioxide levels (the reason why you should use your exhaust fan when cooking on a gas stove and open a window when using an unflued gas heater). In high concentrations VOCs and carbon dioxide can be toxic and carcinogenic and even at low levels may impact our health.

The humble house plant offers a solution. Houseplants absorb these indoor air pollutants, making our homes a healthier place to be. You don't need a forest of pot plants to enjoy the benefits. Research has found as few as three potted plants in an average sized office can reduce VOCs to an extremely low level.[7][8]

You don't need to spend a fortune at a garden centre on houseplants. Instead propagate plants by collecting cuttings from friends' plants. For an idea of plants that are especially easy to propagate, reflect back on the houseplants your grandmother or an old aunt had. My gran had plenty

---

[7] Ronald A Wood et al. 'The Potted-Plant Microcosm Substantially Reduces Indoor Air VOC Pollution: I. Office Field-Study' *Water, Air, and Soil Pollution*, Volume 175, Issue 1-4 September 2006, pp 163-180 http://dx.doi.org/10.1007/s11270-006-9124-z

[8] Editor's Note: Nicole Bijlsma, author of *Healthy Home, Healthy Family*, recommends one plant per square metre on her website. I asked her about the discrepancy, and she replied that 'the number of plants required to effectively improve the air quality depends on several factors (contaminant, surrounding building materials, ventilation, humidity levels, room size etc) which is why there are discrepancies amongst studies as to how many plants are required. However, the point is that they are wonderful as part of any building.' (Personal email, 15 September 2013.)

of african violets which are very easy to propagate from leaf cuttings; spider plants that shoot off teeny plants which can be planted individually; and peace lilies that can easily be divided.

Nor do you need to spend a fortune on pots. Quirky and unique pots can be made from old teapots and casserole dishes by drilling a hole in the bottom for drainage. If the container is terracotta or lightly glazed clay, to drill a hole soak the pot in water, place masking tape over where you want to drill and use a masonry drill bit. If it is heavily glazed or glass, for example old Pyrex casserole dishes, you'll need a fancier diamond-coated drill bit. Expect a few breakages, so don't try this on anything too precious.

Spider Plant, by Trish Hogbin, 2013

[2]

What are Phthalates?

NYREE BEKARIAN

Nyree Bekarian is a senior scientist at Exponent Inc and a contributing writer at Greenopedia.com. She has a Master's degree in Environmental Health Science and has previously worked for Environ International Corporation, the US EPA, and the Center for Children's Environmental Health at the University of California, Berkeley.
http://twitter.com/nyree_1

PHTHALATES REFER TO a family of chemicals used to improve the flexibility and durability of plastics. They have other uses in common consumer goods, including food packaging, home décor, and personal care and beauty products. [9]

COMMON PRODUCTS CONTAINING PHTHALATES

Phthalates are fairly ubiquitous in consumer products and are most commonly used to soften PVC plastics. Consumer

---

[9] EDITOR'S NOTE: Phthalates (pronounced thal-ates) could easily be included in the section on cosmetics or on plastics. But as they are so common, it seemed most appropriate to include Nyree's articles here.

products that typically contain phthalates include:

- highly flexible plasticized materials, such as rain coats and shower curtains
- building materials and home décor, such as water pipes, vinyl flooring, and mini-blinds
- household cleaners, glues, paints, and air fresheners
- children's toys and school supplies, such as lunch boxes and plastic folders
- automobile parts, such as plastic consoles, steering wheels, and vinyl seating
- food packaging, such as plastic wraps and soft plastic food containers
- personal care products, such as soap, shampoo, nail polish, perfume, hair spray, and moisturizer
- other personal items, such as sex toys and first aid products.

ARE THERE ADVERSE EFFECTS OF PHTHALATES?

Phthalates have been shown to cause adverse effects on the lungs, liver, kidneys, and male reproductive system of lab animals. A small number of studies has identified possible links between exposure to phthalates and various reproductive and developmental health effects in humans, including fertility impairment, female reproductive disease, and early puberty in females. Studies have also shown a possible link between exposure to phthalates and both asthma and thyroid disease. In addition, the National Toxicology Program (NTP) concluded that the phthalate DEHP is 'reasonably anticipated to be a human carcinogen'.

All phthalates do not have the same potency or potential effects on our health. Furthermore, the age at which a person is exposed to phthalates plays a role on the severity of the health effects; it's been shown that fetuses and infants are more sensitive than adults.

WHERE AM I EXPOSED TO PHTHALATES?

People are directly exposed to phthalates just by handling products that are made with them. Because phthalates do not bind to plastics, they are easily transferred from a product onto the skin, and either absorbed by the skin or ingested through hand-to-mouth contact. Phthalates can also be released into the air and people can be exposed to airborne phthalates by breathing them in. Certain plastics used in food packaging can contain phthalates, which migrate from packaging into food or beverages and are then ingested. Increased fat content in food and beverages can increase the migration of phthalates from packaging. High heat, like microwaving or placing hot foods in plastic containers, will also increase the migration of phthalates into food or release them into the air.

AVOIDING PHTHALATES IN EVERYDAY ITEMS

Easy ways to reduce exposure to phthalates in everyday items include avoiding products made with PVC plastics and looking for the words 'phthalate-free' or 'fragrance-free' on packaging. Reading ingredient labels is also a good way to check if a product might contain hidden phthalates. Avoid products whose ingredients include 'fragrance' or 'perfume'. Products scented with essential oils are good choices. Reducing phthalate exposure in baby and children's products includes choosing toys and products made from wood, natural fibers, or other non-plastic materials.[10] And while it is nearly impossible to avoid phthalates entirely, there are a few easy ways to reduce phthalate exposure at home by choosing healthier materials and ingredients in everyday purchases.

REFERENCES

Congressional Research Service (CRS). 2008. CRS Report for Congress: Phthalates in Plastics and Possible Human Health Effects. July.

The Lowell Center for Sustainable Production. 2011. Phthalates and Their Alternatives: Health and Environmental Concerns. January.

The National Academy of Sciences. 2008. Phthalates and Cumulative Risk Assessment.

http://www.breastcancerfund.org/clear-science/chemicals-glossary/phthalates.html

http://safecosmetics.org/article.php?id=290

http://www.fda.gov/downloads/Drugs/GuidanceCompliance%20RegulatoryInformation/Guidances/UCM294086.pdf

http://dels.nas.edu/resources/static-assets/materials-based-on-reports/reports-in-brief/phthalates_final.pdf

http://www.niehs.nih.gov/research/supported/assets/docs/j_q/phthalates_the_everywhere_chemical_handout_.pdf

---

[10] See also 'Phthalates in baby and children's products' by Nyree Bekarian: http://greenopedia.com/article/phthalates-baby-and-children%E2%80%99s-products

[3]

Easy Ways to Reduce Phthalate Exposure

NYREE BEKARIAN

Nyree Bekarian is a senior scientist at Exponent Inc and a contributing writer at Greenopedia.com. She has a Master's degree in Environmental Health Science and has previously worked for Environ International Corporation, the US EPA, and the Center for Children's Environmental Health at the University of California, Berkeley.
http://twitter.com/nyree_1

PHTHALATES ARE FOUND in thousands of consumer products and have been linked to adverse human and animal health effects. Phthalates are so widespread that they are nearly impossible to avoid completely, but there are some easy ways to reduce exposure.

REDUCE PHTHALATE EXPOSURE IN FOOD

Phthalates are found in plastics made from polyvinyl chloride (PVC). These plastics, stamped with recycling code 3, are often used to package processed and premade foods. Choosing food and drink packaged in non-PVC plastics, such as polyethylene terephthalate (PETE), high density polyethylene (HDPE), and polypropylene (PP) (recycling codes 1, 2, and 5, respectively) is a good way to reduce phthalate exposure from packaged foods.[11]

Preparing your own meals using fresh foods greatly reduces the risk of phthalate exposure from plastic food packaging. Storing and reheating food or drink in glass, ceramic or stainless steel, instead of plastic or plastic wrap, further reduces exposure.

REDUCE PHTHALATE EXPOSURE IN PERSONAL CARE ITEMS

There are several uses for phthalates in personal care products. Phthalates increase the durability of nail polish, reduce stiffness in hairspray, and increase the effectiveness of moisturizers. Phthalates are also used to help blend fragrance mixtures and stabilize fragrances to help them last longer. Lotions, cleansers, scented candles, laundry detergents and other personal care and household products that list 'fragrance', 'perfume' or even 'natural fragrance' as ingredients often contain phthalates. To reduce exposure to phthalates through personal care products, choose products that are labeled as 'phthalate-free' or that are scented only with essential oils.

Phthalate-free nail polishes are becoming easier to find in the marketplace. Many nail salons now carry phthalate-

---

[11] See Chapter 19 'What do the numbers on plastics mean?'

free polishes and many of those that don't, allow clients to bring in their own phthalate-free polish.

PHTHALATE EXPOSURE IN COMMON HOUSEHOLD ITEMS

Phthalates are commonly found in synthetic air fresheners, including spray, gel, and plug-in varieties. Those that claim 'all natural ingredients' may still contain phthalates. Flowers, potpourri (without synthetic additives), or an open window are healthier ways to freshen your home.

Vinyl shower curtains and shower curtain liners often contain phthalates, and heat from a shower could increase their release into the air. Shower curtains and liners made from cloth or those labeled as 'phthalate-free' or 'PVC-free' are safer alternatives to conventional, vinyl shower curtains and liners.

Vinyl flooring and window treatments are typically made from PVC plastics. Window treatments made from natural materials, such as curtains made from cotton or linen and blinds made from wood or bamboo are a healthier alternative to those made from vinyl. Selecting flooring made from natural materials like wood, bamboo, or natural linoleum can further reduce phthalate exposures at home.

Concerned parents with babies or small children can reduce exposures to phthalates by covering vinyl flooring with a sheet or quilted mat before allowing children to crawl or play on it. This will reduce dermal exposure, but not inhalation exposure, to phthalates. Soft 'rubber' play mats are often made from PVC plastics and should be avoided to reduce phthalate exposure.[12]

REFERENCES

Congressional Research Service (CRS). 2008. CRS Report for Congress: Phthalates in Plastics and Possible Human Health Effects. July.

The Lowell Center for Sustainable Production. 2011. Phthalates and Their Alternatives: Health and Environmental Concerns. January.

The National Academy of Sciences. 2008. Phthalates and Cumulative Risk Assessment.

http://www.breastcancerfund.org/clear-science/chemicals-glossary/phthalates.html

---

[12] See also 'Phthalates in baby and children's products' by Nyree Bekarian: http://greenopedia.com/article/phthalates-baby-and-children%E2%80%99s-products

[4]

Six Reasons to Leave Your Shoes at the Door

JO HEGERTY

Jo Hegerty is a journalist and copywriter passionate about inspiring small changes with big outcomes. She writes an eco-living blog for busy mums, and wrangles two kids, four chickens and a lively cattle dog in suburban Queensland. For tips and ideas on how to green your life, visit: http://www.downtoearthmother.com

IN MANY PARTS of Asia, no-one would think about tramping around their home—or someone else's for that matter—with their shoes on. You just need to take a walk down a slippery Bangkok street or dodge phlegm-oysters in Chongqing to understand why slippers are the norm indoors. Some people even have little plastic covers to slip over your feet to save honoured guests the hassle of removing their shoes.

No matter how clean our streets look in our corner of civilisation, there are a whole lot of good reasons to leave the outdoors at the door. Naturopath and author of *Healthy*

Home, Healthy Family, Nicole Bijlsma, lists removing your shoes as the first of seven steps you can take to dramatically reduce the number of toxins in your home.[13]

It may seem a hassle, but taking off your shoes quickly becomes a habit. We have a shoe rack at the front door and a selection of old thongs and shoes that have been delegated to garden wear at the back door. I tend to run in and out of the house fifty million times a day and barely break stride as I slip in and out of my shoes.

Here are six reasons to leave your shoes at the door:

DUST: According to Nicole, removing your shoes can reduce dust in your home by at least 50 per cent.

GRIME: Professional home cleaners estimate that a whopping 85 per cent of grime on the floors and carpet is tracked in on the soles of your shoes and the paws of pets. One of the major benefits of not allowing shoes in the house is that you don't need to clean the floors as often, woohoo!

LEAD: The EPA recommends taking shoes off to reduce the occurrence of lead in homes. Lead is found in the soil in many areas, especially around the perimeters of older homes where lead-paint chips have fallen to the ground and deteriorated. Very small amounts of lead can cause significant health problems, especially to small children.

PESTICIDES: Studies have shown that pesticide residue can cling to shoes for up to a week after application. Even if you don't spray your lawn, public areas and parks are likely to be treated.

---

[13] See http://www.buildingbiology.com.au for the other 6 steps.

ALLERGENS: If you suffer allergies, you probably already know that by leaving your shoes on, you're bringing the problem inside!

PEACE: Another great reason for a shoe-free home is that it separates your sanctuary from the world outside. Symbolically, it says 'this is my space'. It sounds wanky, but it really does have an impact. I find it really weird to sit on a couch with shoes on my feet—it just feels wrong!

[5]

Are Your Candles Killing You and Harming the Planet?

CATE BURTON

Cate is a long term devotee of sustainable, chemical free living and to that end, set up Queen B Beeswax Candles over a decade ago. In her spare time she's a keen balcony veggie gardener and urban beekeeping enthusiast (with 2 beehives on her balcony) and runs Bees In The City.
http://www.queenb.com.au

AS OUR ORIGINAL source of light, candles have played a role in human civilisation for centuries. Initially used to 'prolong the day' and lengthen available working hours, in modern life their use is almost the opposite. Candles are used to facilitate relaxation, create romance, imbue ambience, symbolise celebration, focus meditation and complement décor. A signal to our frazzled psyche that the day is over.

29

There are four types of wax from which candles are made in modern times. In order of volume of production they are: paraffin, soy, palm and beeswax.

PARAFFIN

The vast majority of candles sold are made from paraffin because it is the cheapest wax available. Paraffin costs around 1/50th of the price of 100 percent pure Australian beeswax when bought in bulk. Unless a candle is otherwise labelled, it will be made from paraffin. That said even candles labelled 'beeswax' might contain up to 90 percent paraffin.[14]

Paraffin is a toxic waste product from petroleum refining. This grayish-black sludge is bleached with 100 per cent pure bleach (the bleach used in laundries is about 10 per cent), creating billions of tonnes of dioxins. The discovery of paraffin revolutionised candle-making because it was cheap and readily available. Still is.

As a toxic product, paraffin is shipped to the candle factory with a Material Safety Data Sheet (MSDS).[15] Concerningly, the MSDS says that when handling paraffin (and this is while it is in an 'inert'—ie unlit—form) you need to wear gloves, a lab coat, goggles and a respirator!

To turn the paraffin into a candle, it is generally dyed (with chemical dyes), fragranced (with synthetic, petrochemical fragrant oils), poured in a mould, over-packaged

---

[14] Indeed, a Melbourne based candle company produces candles labelled 'Beeswax', but when you call and ask what percentage beeswax they are, they advise that it is less than 20 per cent.

[15] You can google 'paraffin MSDS' to see one for yourself.

and shipped out to unsuspecting buyers... and the MSDS is missing.

The toxicity of burning paraffin candles has been known for many years. As with chemicals in cosmetics and skincare however, there is little regulation and manufacturing continues unabated. Industry regulations do not require candle manufacturers and retailers to disclose hazardous compounds, or to provide a comprehensive ingredient list, even upon consumer request.

According to recent research by Ruhullah Massoudi and Amid Hamidi, scientists from South Carolina State University, 'Each time a candle is burned, if it is paraffin, which is basically petroleum-based, it provides really nasty chemicals in the emissions'. As part of the research, candles were burned in a special chamber with the contents of the smoke monitored and measured. They found that benzene, toluene and ketones were present in the smoke.[16] The Environmental Protection Agency (EPA) has determined that benzene and toluene are probable human carcinogens.

In addition, many paraffin candles are made with a lead core or zinc core wick, adding to the toxicity of the smoke emissions. Whilst lead core wicks have been banned in Australia, there have been several instances of imported candles being found on sale with these wicks, even since the ban. Candles with a zinc core are not banned and continue to be sold in Australia. They are commonly used in scented candles.

---

[16] Benzene has been linked to bone marrow failure disorders like aplastic anemia, myelodysplastic syndromes, and acute lymphocytic leukemia. Toluene and ketones are associated with asthma and birth defects.

A University of Michigan study found that wicks that have lead cores, or zinc cores contaminated with lead, emit potentially dangerous levels of lead into the air—including allergens and carcinogens such as benzene, acetone, mercury and toluene. The effects of these emissions can be damaging to the cardiovascular, neurological and immune systems. The scientist concluded 'burning leaded candles can result in extensive contamination of the air and house dust with lead.'[17]

A similar study was conducted in Australia by Mike van Alphen from The Lead Group which summed up

'Modelling of a number of residential scenarios and detailed exposure assessments readily demonstrate that daily candle burning of several hours duration would result in elevated blood lead levels. The burning of multiple candles in a confined space for greater than 3-6 hours daily would readily result in severe Pb poisoning.'[18]

SOY & PALM

I have grouped these candles together because the issues with them are largely the same. Manufacturers of these types of candles will try to differentiate them, and focus on them being 'natural waxes', but if you're going to be pedantic about

---

[17] Jerome Nriagu quoted in Amy Reyes, 'Some candles with lead wicks emit lead into the air' The University of Michigan News and Information Services, October 1999, http://www.ns.umich.edu/Releases/1999/Oct99/r100699.html

[18] See Mike van Alphen, 'Killer Candles', The Lead Group Inc., 1999, http://www.lead.org.au/mr/9-8-99.html. Editor's note: This article also gives simple instructions for detecting lead cores.

it and play on words, paraffin is a natural wax in that petroleum is 'natural'. It doesn't mean that we want it burning in our lounge rooms. Arm yourself with facts, not marketing.

Both soy and palm are oils when harvested—soya bean oil and palm oil respectively. To turn them into a wax they are bleached (creating billions of tonnes of dioxins) and then hydrogenated. I may be unusual, but to me something is 'natural' when it is used in the form it is harvested, not when it is so altered by chemical processes that it doesn't bear any resemblance to the harvested product.

This hydrogenated soy oil/palm oil is then typically coloured and scented. There is no research that I know of that examines the emissions created by dyeing/colouring a candle. There is, however, research that confirms that scenting a candle creates toxic emissions when burning. This is discussed later in the article.

The other major issue with soy and palm is that both of them are cash crops primarily grown in third world countries where the lack of corporate governance and incidence of corruption is rife leading to the clear felling of millions of hectares of virgin rainforest annually.

According to a report by Greenpeace,

> 'The Amazon Rainforest is the largest expanse of tropical rainforest in the world, but it is disappearing at an alarming rate—since the 1970s, an area of rainforest the size of California has been lost. Few people today realize that the greatest threat facing the Amazon is the production of soy.'[19]

---

[19] Greenpeace, 'Nothing YUMmy About Amazon Destruction' 18 May 2006

A World Wildlife Fund study on the impacts of soybean cultivation in Brazil by environmental analyst Jan Maarten Dros said 'Soy – at this moment – is the most important driver for deforestation, directly and indirectly.'[20]

The wanton destruction of virgin rainforests is not, however, limited to Brazil. According to the National Directorate of Forests, Argentina is experiencing the most intense deforestation in its history due to the replacement of forests with soy plantations.

'Over the past decade, as the output of soy rose steadily, the province [of Córdoba] lost an average of three per cent of its native forests annually. Of the 10 million hectares of forests found in Córdoba a century ago, only 12 per cent are left.'[21]

In our own backyard, South East Asia, the issues are largely duplicated but this time the culprit is palm plantations. As said by the Mark Forbes in the Sydney Morning Herald:

'Clearing peat forests has made Indonesia the world's third-largest greenhouse gas emitter, sending more than 3000-million tonnes of carbon dioxide into the atmosphere a year. It is driven by greed, with palm oil and timber barons lining the pockets of officials from Kalimantan to Jakarta'.[22]

---

[20] Quoted in CorpWatch, 'Paving the Amazon with Soy', by Sasha Lilley, 16 December 2004, http://www.corpwatch.org/article.php?id=11756

[21] Inter Press Service News Agency, 'More Soy, Less Forest - and No Water', by Marcela Valente

[22] Mark Forbes (Indonesia Correspondent Kalimantan), 'Up in the trees, the boss hangs on for a miracle' Sydney Morning Herald, 1 December 2007

After logging rainforest habitat, palm oil companies often use uncontrolled burning to clear the land. In 1997-98 a devastating fire killed almost 8,000 orangutans in Borneo. Orangutans are predicted to be extinct in the wild in the next 20 years if the palm oil industry, deforestation and burning of peat forest do not change. In February 2007 the situation for the Orangutans was called a state of emergency by the United Nations.[24]

BEESWAX

The fourth, and least common, wax used to make candles is beeswax. Pure Australian beeswax costs around 50 times the price of bulk paraffin and 20 times the price of hydrogenated soy or palm oil. That said Australian beeswax is the most expensive beeswax in the world.[25] There are certainly cheaper beeswaxes available.

Beeswax is made by bees to store honey. It is completely natural—in the sense that you and I know 'natural' to be—it is used in the form it is harvested. It is not chemically treated and processed to create a wax.

There are a couple of other qualities of beeswax that make it a superior wax for candle-making. The first is that beeswax has the highest melting point of any wax known to humankind. Whereas you will often find that paraffin candles drip or drown the wick, and soy or palm candles typically

---

[24] United Nations Environment Programme (UNEP) in their report 'Last Stand of the Orangutan'

[25] The main reason for this is because Australian beeswax is free from the chemical residues found in beeswax from other countries because our hives do not have to be chemically treated for the varroa mite.

come in jars or have hardeners such as stearic acid added to the wax, a beeswax candle (when properly made) will not drown the wick and rarely drips.[26] Beeswax also has a natural, light honey aroma without being artificially scented.

The other unique thing about beeswax is that it is purported to be a natural ioniser when burning. Rather than buying an electric ioniser to purify the air you breathe, by simply lighting a pure beeswax candle it emits negative ions. The negative ions then attach to the positive ions floating in the air (dust, germs, viruses, aromas etc) making them heavier and causing them to drop to the ground.

I must admit to being completely biased. In the interests of complete transparency, I declare that I am a beeswax candle-maker. Having said that, I am biased because I have researched waxes and candles extensively and that shows that the only candles that are non-toxic to burn and carbon neutral are 100 percent pure beeswax candles.[27] This article seeks to share with you about 1/100th of the research that I have done myself (all of it consistent) in making my decision to stick to making pure Australian beeswax candles.

The major reason why there aren't many beeswax candles available is because running a business making pure Australian beeswax candles is spectacularly unprofitable! Whilst our wax costs 20—50 times the price of paraffin and soy/palm, customers (who are still largely uneducated about

---

[26] The major exception to this rule is if the candle is burning in a breeze—which makes the flamer larger and melts the wax quicker and may lead to some dripping.

[27] The carbon neutrality of pure beeswax candles is stated by the organisers of Earth Hour globally, the World Wildlife Fund.

candles) aren't prepared to pay that. That makes beeswax candle-making financially challenging. However, it is incredibly rewarding in a myriad of other ways.

I decided to stand up and be counted. I decided it was worthwhile making candles that were truly non-toxic, that caused no environmental damage, that would support Australian beekeepers and the regional communities in which they live, and create jobs in Australia. I would be financially rich if I took the advice of, or had a dollar for, each well-meaning accountant, friend, small business expert or business consultant who told me that in order to make Queen B profitable I needed to move production offshore, import beeswax and/or blend the beeswax with a cheaper wax or oil. I am rich in other ways for choosing not to.

Next time you light a candle in your living space, consider what it is doing to you and the planet.

SIDE NOTE—SCENTED CANDLES

Another phenomenon worthy of close examination is scented candles. With the rise in popularity of aromatherapy in the past decade, candle-makers have begun scenting candles.

The vast majority of candles are scented with fragrant oils. Fragrance oils (also known as aroma oils, aromatic oils and flavour oils) are blended synthetic aroma compounds that are then diluted with a carrier such as propylene glycol, vegetable oil or mineral oil.[28] Mineral oil is, of course, another petrochemical. These are fragrances created in a

---

[28] See http://en.wikipedia.org/wiki/Fragrance_oil

laboratory—there is little that is 'natural' about them. Candle-makers prefer to use fragrant oils because they are considerably cheaper than essential oils and they are also typically less volatile.

Some candle-makers do, however, use essential oils. The issue here is that essential oils are naturally high in volatile organic compounds (VOCs) and should not be 'combusted'. It is perfectly safe to use an oil burner whereby you put a few drops of essential oil in water that is then warmed and the essential oil vapourises. It is not safe to combust an essential oil which is what you are doing when you scent a candle—ie you pour the oil directly into the molten wax when manufacturing. This wax and oil is then drawn up the wick to fuel the flame where it combusts. The smoke from burning essential oils may contain potential carcinogens, such as polycyclic aromatic hydrocarbons (PAHs).[29]

Many of the common essential oils such as tea tree, lavender, and citrus oils are classed as a HAZMAT Class 3 Flammable Liquid as they have a flash point of 50–60 °C.[30]

---

[29] Essential Oil Encyclopaedia. See also the MSDS from essential oils, eg http://www.newdirectionsaromatics.com/msds/peppermintgeraniummsds.htm

[30] See http://en.wikipedia.org/wiki/Essential_oil

[6]

Detoxify Your Medicine Cabinet

DR TERAY GARCHITORENA KUNISHI

Dr. Teray Garchitorena Kunishi, ND is co-founder of the Berkeley Naturopathic Medical Group in Berkeley, California. Her workshops and programs provide solutions for depression, anxiety, fatigue, chronic stress and insomnia, ADHD and PTSD.
http://www.berkeleynaturopathic.com

HEADACHE MEDICATION:

Headaches have many causes, from tension, stress, dehydration, and environmental sensitivity to food intolerance, to name a few. While over the counter medications like aspirin, ibuprofen and acetaminophen can stop the ache, overuse of these medications can harm the digestive tract and even cause liver damage.

What's a non-toxic family to do? Following are some suggestions.

1. A few drops of lavender essential oil in a jojoba oil base can do wonders to head off a headache in its early stages. Rub over temples and forehead, inhale deeply and feel the tension melt away.

2. Make sure to stay hydrated. A simple way to calculate how much water one should drink is to take your weight in pounds and divide by two. Then take that number and drink it in fluid ounces. So a 160 pound person would drink 80 ounces daily, which is about 2.4 litres—this includes soups, caffeine free teas and unsweetened drinks.

3. For many people, food and environmental sensitivities and allergies can trigger migraines. Common food culprits are preservatives, alcohol, sugar, gluten and dairy. Fragrances can trigger headaches as well so going scent-free can be a blessing for headache sufferers.

4. Feverfew—(Tanacetum parthenium L)—Feverfew reduces inflammation, supports blood vessels and controls allergy symptoms.

5. Purple Butterbur (Petasites hybridus)—Butterbur has been found to reduce the frequency of migraines. It does this by helping blood vessels to maintain a healthy tone. It is also effective for reducing the severity of allergies. Only butterbur products that have been processed to remove pyrrolizidine alkaloids and are labeled or certified as PA-free should be used.

6. Magnesium—this mineral relaxes the muscles and also helps calm the nervous system down,

making it an important ally in keeping headaches and tension at bay.

7. Riboflavin—Also known as B2, this important vitamin acts as an antioxidant and helps other vitamins like folate work better. People who take riboflavin tend to have fewer migraine headaches.

ANTIHISTAMINES:

Diphenhydramine and chlorpheniramine are popular over the counter allergy medications, but they often cause drowsiness.

It's important to note that even seasonal allergies can become less severe when food intolerances and food sensitivities are avoided.

While you figure that part out, here are some alternatives to help keep seasonal allergies at bay:

1. Neti Lota Pot—Ayurveda has long prescribed using salt water to rinse out the sinuses as a part of daily hygiene. A simple solution made with sea salt and warm filtered water helps wash away allergens, soothe the nasal cavities and block viruses from taking hold. It feels a little odd to pour water into one nostril and watch it trickle out the other, but with practice, it is quite comfortable.

   For the less adventurous, a regular saline nasal spray from the chemist (drugstore) works well too.

2. Quercitin—this bioflavonoid, found in onions and other plant foods, seems to help control the release of histamine, the main culprit in allergy

symptoms. Look for quercetin in combination with nettles and vitamin C for the synergistic prevention of the sniffles.

For best results, natural allergy treatments should start three weeks before allergy season.

COUGH MEDICINE

Dextromethopan is the most common medicine used for coughs. Researchers have found that, while popular, it doesn't actually work for acute coughs.

NATURAL COUGH RELIEF:

HONEY—this simple and delicious home remedy has proven to be effective for helping children sleep better with a cough.

COFFEE—A surprising study showed that a jam-like combination of honey and coffee controlled that nagging post-flu cough better than steroids or guaifenesin.[31]

Here is the formula: 20.8g of honey and 2.9g of instant coffee in warm water three times daily for about a week.

This information is for educational purposes only. It is not meant to diagnose, treat or prevent illness. Always consult your doctor before changing your medication.

---

[31] Mohammad Ali Raeessi, Jafar Aslani, et al. 'Honey plus coffee versus systemic steroid in the treatment of persistent post-infectious cough: a randomised controlled trial' *Prim Care Respir J* 2013;22(3):325-330. DOI: http://dx.doi.org/10.4104/pcrj.2013.00072

[7]

Is It OK to Ingest Essential Oils?

KATHARINE KOEPPEN

Katharine Koeppen, RA, LMT, NCTMB, is a US nationally registered aromatherapist, seasoned clinician, author and educator with twenty years in aromatic practice. An avid writer and blogger, her work has been published internationally by professional aromatherapy associations, magazines and peer-reviewed journals. Katharine may be found online at: http://www.aromaceuticals.com

I'VE BEEN ASKED this question often lately, and the queries have come from both healthcare professionals and consumers. This is an issue which concerns me greatly, because oral ingestion is heavily promoted by several multi-level marketing essential oil companies in an attempt to sell their products. Such companies appear to focus on sales rather than education and safety, and the average person who attends their presentations does not understand that essential oils can be potentially misused... and by far the easiest way to misuse these fragrant substances is through oral ingestion.

British and American aromatherapy deals with application of essential oils via inhalation or topically in dilute form. When applied in this manner, the oils initially bypass the liver and engage with various cellular structures and neurotransmitters to have the desired effect on the body. Ultimately, the metabolites of these essential oils leave cells, are taken up by blood and lymph, recirculate in the body, are processed through the liver, and finally excreted through the urinary or intestinal systems. By the time the oils or their metabolites leave the liver, they have largely done their job.

Not so with oral ingestion. In this case, essential oils may have time to act upon some digestive system issues, but by the time they reach the small intestine, they are absorbed into the circulatory system and taken up by the liver. There, they are broken down into various phytochemicals, which are then further metabolized. Problems can occur when the liver decides it prefers to process other substances first, and phytochemicals accumulate in line waiting to be processed, sometimes accumulating in toxic amounts. For example, the liver doesn't 'like' 1,8 cineole, a common bioactive fraction of peppermint, tea tree, niaouli and many eucalypts. Taken orally in improper doses, 1,8 cineole can quickly accumulate to the point where it causes liver failure. In a child, less than 2 milliliters are a deadly dose. In an individual with compromised liver function, even small amounts of oils containing 1,8 cineole taken orally can cause dangerously elevated liver enzymes in a matter of a few days.

There is also the matter of drug interactions. All essential oils have some sort of effect upon P450 liver detoxification enzymes. Some inhibit or accelerate phase 1 enzymes, some inhibit or accelerate phase 2 enzymes, and still some interact with both phase 1 and 2 enzymes. This does not pose a problem with the majority of essential oils when inhalation therapy or topical application is used, but does create problems with oral ingestion. If a pharmaceutical medication has a narrow therapeutic window, it is undesirable (and may be downright dangerous) to limit the effectiveness of the drug by slowing or speeding up the way it is processed in the body.

There are different protocols for ingesting essential oils, depending on the part of the body that the aromatherapy needs to target. If you don't know these protocols, don't take essential oils orally. Taking oils incorrectly may cause burning of the mucous membranes of the mouth and throat, upset stomach, heartburn, diarrhea, or may be altogether ineffective.

A surprising number of consumers believe that all natural remedies are safe, and see no problem using essential oils with abandon. A person who would never consider taking half a bottle of aspirin in a sitting has no problem downing a teaspoon of highly concentrated essential oil. Unbelievably, these people do exist... and I've written about them previously on my blog in posts on grapefruit[32] and peppermint[33] oil abuse.

---

[32] Katharine Koeppen 'Is Grapefruit Oil a "Fat Burner"?' (2011) http://www.aromaceuticals.com/blog/is-grapefruit-oil-a-fat-burner

[33] Katharine Koeppen 'Adverse Reactions to Peppermint Oil' (2011) http://www.aromaceuticals.com/blog/adverse-reactions-to-peppermint-oil

Unless you have the time and energy to devote to your own serious research, or wish to invest in classes covering aromachemistry, pharmacology, anatomy and physiology, don't experiment with ingesting essential oils. If you find this suggestion intimidating and still feel you must take aromatics orally, book a consultation with a qualified clinical aromatherapist for guidance.

[8]

My Simple Home: Earthing Mats

SARAH WILSON

Sarah Wilson is a journalist and TV presenter who writes about 'how to make life better'. She describes herself as on a mission to find ways to make life bigger, more meaningful, nicer, smarter, healthier. Sarah is the author of the recently released best-seller I Quit Sugar. *http://sarahwilson.com.au*

BRACE YOURSELVES, TEAM. We're heading into the kind of territory that brings folk out of the woodwork to throw the usual cries of 'but where's the vacuum-sealed, octo-blind, inreverse placebo, set-in-concrete scientifical study that proves what you say beyond a doubt?!' Yes, now we're going to discuss earthing mats. Which sound like something that a dude in fisherman pants and a child called Forest Pxyiee would try to sell you, right?

Admittedly I did first hear about the idea while I was living in Byron Bay. And it was a dude in fisherman pants who waxed lyrical about it while toting a chai. A few months back, however, building biologist Nicole Bijlsma[34] brought the idea and the mats up again when she did a toxin audit on my home. She claims the mats will reduce body voltage created by the electric fields around you, and are particularly good for those who have electric hypersensitivity (EHS).[35] You can see the video chats we did in my home on my website[36][37] where we discuss the various sources of electromagnetic fields (EMF) in the house and the solutions you can put in place to minimise them.

In a (cracked?) nut the idea behind earthing, however, is this:

The earth has a negative grounding charge. We humans build up positive electrons (free radicals) from EMFs, Wi-Fi etc.

Connecting directly with the earth equalizes things.

To earth is simply to walk barefoot on dirt or beach or grass. The effect is much like grounding electrical outlets to prevent build up of positive electrical charge. Health benefits, calmness, good sleep ensue.

---

[34] See About the Contributors, p. 185

[35] Nicole Bijlsma 'Electromagnetic fields - we live in a sea of radiation' http://www.buildingbiology.com.au/index.php/Biology/Electromagnetic-Fields.html

[36] Sarah Wilson 'How to detox your kitchen' http://www.sarahwilson.com.au/2013/02/my-simple-home-how-to-detox-your-kitchen

[37] Sarah Wilson 'Five small hazards to avoid' http://www.sarahwilson.com.au/2013/03/my-simple-home-5-small-hazards-to-avoid

HOW TO EARTH:

- Walk barefoot. While we used to connect via our bare feet, now we have a layer of rubber between us and the earth, which insulates and prevents the grounding transfer. Get your shoes off and walk in a park on the grass or dirt, or along a beach.
- Walk on the beach. Wondered why you come back from a beach stroll so anchored and calm? Sand and salt water are particularly conductive and earth us even more effectively.
- Use an earthing mat under your bed. This is what Nicole got me onto. An earthing mat, or sheet, is like a short undersheet that you place on top of your bottom sheet (it needs skin contact to work), with a cord that connects to a socket in the wall. The electrons from the earth will flow up (regardless of whether your home is on the ground floor or the 12th floor) through the ground wires and onto the mat, and earth you. While you sleep.
- Use an earthing mat under your computer. This is a small rubber mat connected to a wall socket. It works to the same principles above: Electrons will flow up/through your building and onto the mat. Ergo, keeping you grounded while you work.

WHAT ON EARTH DOES IT DO?

The claim is that grounding or earthing has a bunch of health benefits, including reducing inflammation (thus helping with auto-immune conditions), reducing chronic pain, helping with jet lag, balancing out hormonal issues and most importantly to me, improving sleep by normalizing your biological circadian rhythms. I kinda get it. On beach holidays I always sleep better. When I feel grounded and unfrazzled, I sleep better.

WHERE'S THE PROOF?

Yes, yes, I can hear the troll-y skeptics rumbling in the ranks. It appears there are a bunch of preliminary studies that have been done on the subject, which are outlined on http://radianthealthtoday.com.[38] They're far from gold standard and the results are not conclusive. But, as I ask often, are they ever? And can you imagine earthing mat research getting a stack of funding?

I also saw a photo on Wellness Mama's blog a while back.[39] Thermographic imaging had been used to show how earthing can affect inflammation. The image was taken of a woman who complained of stiffness and chronic pain. The first picture was taken before earthing, and the second, after just 30 minutes of earthing. The difference was startling. I can't vouch for its pristine scientific credentials. But I find it intriguing.

---

[38] Logan Christopher 'Get Grounded: The Benefits of Maintaining a Connection to the Earth' http://radianthealthtoday.com/GroundingReport.pdf

[39] Katie WellnessMama 'How to Get Healthy While You Sleep' *Wellness Mama* http://wellnessmama.com/5600/how-to-get-healthy-while-you-sleep

DOES GROUNDING WORK?

As always with this kind of thing, I prefer to test things out for myself. The claims pertaining to inflammation and sleep were too enticing for me not to give the mats a crack. Obviously it's a study of one. You draw your own conclusions.

THE COMPUTER MAT: I place it under my feet while I work (with bare feet). It's hard to say if it's had a direct effect, but I can say that overall my inflammation has been better the past few months. Coincidence? Hard to say when your health is a cluster of symptoms. I try not to get too attached to devices like this, too attached to a miraculous outcome. I think I'm going to pass it on to friends to see if they can notice a discernible effect (and meantime I'll notice if there's a negative effect from not having it under my feet).

THE BED MAT: I've had the sheet on my bed for two months now. As I've written before,[40] I've been having terrible sleep issues lately, due to a range of factors. Feeling frazzled with pent up 'positive electric energy' ain't my only issue. However, since using the mat I have been waking with less pain in my legs from the inflammation. I tested things by removing the mat for two weeks: the achy pain returned. Also, I've had less cramps and restless legs during the night.

SITTING IN DIRT: I try to meditate outside most mornings (at the end of my walk back from the pool, or after one of my bushruns or at the end of a frenetic day) and sit on a

---

[40] Sarah Wilson 'I'm an insomniac, get me out of here' 16 January 2013, http://www.sarahwilson.com.au/2013/01/im-aninsomniac-get-me-out-of-here/

rock or sand or a lawn in a nearby park. I've always intuitively done this—it makes for a more focused meditation. Since being exposed to this thinking, though, I've been aware of getting my shoes off more often. And getting to the beach at least twice a week. I can tell you that doing so categorically works for me. Try the mats. Or get to a beach.

If you're interested in learning more, you can buy both mats in Australia, as well as the definitive book on topic, *Earthing: The Most Important Health Discovery Ever?*, via Earthing Oz.[41]

---

[41] http://www.earthingoz.com.au/online-store/sleep-systems

CLEANING

[9]

What is Really Lurking Under Your Sink?

KIRSTEN MCCULLOCH

Kirsten McCulloch is the editor of this book and an Australian writer passionate about living a more sustainable, healthy life—for herself, her family and the planet. She writes about non-toxic cleaning and other aspects of a healthy home at Sustainable Suburbia, where you can download her free Non-toxic Cleaning Printables.
http://SustainableSuburbia.net

YOU KNOW YOU should probably switch to non-toxic cleaners, but without the nitty gritty of why, it's hard to hustle up the motivation. After all, the cleaners you buy usually say they're 'green' or 'natural', so they can't be all bad, right?

I mean, those ones aren't giving you cancer or anything, are they?

The bad news is, they actually can be all bad. And even if they're not, they may be mostly bad. Green-washing is rife, and 'natural' does not mean non-toxic, or even environmentally sound. It might mean, for instance, that added to the chemical cocktail, your cleaning product contains .02 per cent organic essential oils. Excellent. The term 'fragrance' can hide a lot of nasty chemicals. But now can we get rid of the rest of the chemical cocktail please?

Here are some startling figures:

> Over 80,000 chemicals are now registered for use in Australia (40,000 industrial chemicals) and accessed via everyday consumer products including foods and food packaging, clothing, building materials, water, cleaning products, personal care products. Yet 75 per cent of these have never been tested for their toxicity on the human body or the environment.[42]

Seventy-five per cent have never been tested for safety. What the?

The problem is, the toxicity of these chemicals—even the ones that have been tested—is not necessarily immediately obvious. Some of them affect some people acutely, with things like headaches, asthma attacks and irritability. But the most concerning effects generally are the long term ones. The ones that are made worse by years of exposure in numerous products, and sometimes to the interaction of different chemicals, so that we can't easily trace them back to a single offender.

And in a lot of cases, the science simply isn't done yet, so we just don't know how safe—or not—these chemicals are.

---

[42] Public Health Association of Australia, Environmental Exposure and Human Health Policy, http://www.phaa.net.au/ policyStatementsInterim.php, viewed 25 September 2013.

The good news is, making your own DIY cleaners, ones that really work and don't have these harmful chemicals, is actually quite straight forward.

Ready for some more bad news? Okay, I'm going to tell you about some of the ingredients your everyday cleaners likely contain (if you haven't made the switch already), and what they can do to you and your family. If this is all too much, just skip ahead to the next chapter, to learn how to make your own.

WHAT ARE THE PRODUCTS YOU USE DAILY DO- ING TO YOUR HEALTH?

DISHWASHING LIQUID

Most commercial dishwashing liquids contain 'fragrance'. You might wonder what that means, since a fragrance can contain anything from dozens to hundreds of synthetic chemicals. Unfortunately, it's impossible to know just what they are, since fragrances, or 'parfums' are considered trade secrets, and ingredients don't need to be listed.

However, we do know that fragrances are a common cause of sensitivities and acute reactions such as head-aches, migraines, coughing, wheezing, skin rashes and irritation. They've also been linked to behavioural change.[43]

There are 4000 chemicals that the word 'fragrance' can include. In a 1989 study, the US National Institute of

---

[43] Bill Statham & Lindy Schneider, *The Chemical Maze: Bookshelf Companion*, Possibility.com, 2012, p.209.

Occupational Health and Safety evaluated 2983 fragrance chemicals and found that 884 were toxic.[44]

Most commercial dishwashing liquids also contain SLES (sodium lauryl ether sulphate[45]) a surfactant (meaning it helps dissolve oils and hold dirt in suspension so it doesn't just resettle on your dishes). Unfortunately, SLES can also be contaminated with 1,4-dioxane and ethylene oxide, potential carcinogens.

> 'Dioxane... happens to be one of the most potent synthetic carcinogens ever studied [and] causes damage to development, reproduction, and the immune and endocrine systems at infinitesimally low doses (in the low parts per trillion). Toxicological studies have not been able to establish a 'threshold' dose below which dioxane does not cause biological impacts.'[46]

According to *The Chemical Maze* most dishwashing liquids also contain petroleum based dyes, some of which are known carcinogens, and which can penetrate the skin.[47] And of the 11 other chemicals *The Chemical Maze* lists as common in dishwashing liquids, nine get the book's second worst rating (a single sad face), meaning best avoided (no double sad faces here though!).

---

[44] Sarah Lantz, *Chemical Free Kids*, 2nd Edition, 2012, p. 92.

[45] Also called sodium laureth sulphate, this is different to sodium lauryl sulphate (SLS), though neither one is great.

[46] Karen Ashton & Elizabeth Salter Green, *The Toxic Consumer: healthy Living in a Hazardous World*, Sterling, NY, 2008, p. 76.

[47] Statham & Schneider, 2012, p.208.

AUTOMATIC DISHWASHER POWDER

'Dishwasher powder is one of the five most common causes of accidental poisonings of young children in the home.'[48]

Dishwasher powder can contain chlorine, which means the steam that leaks out of your dishwasher can include chlorine gas, along with that artificial fragrance. Common ingredients listed in *The Chemical Maze* include two that get the double sad face (ie the worst rating): benzotriazole and nitrilotriacetic acid, which is banned in the US. Both are harmful if swallowed, the former is suspected of respiratory and neurotoxicity, the latter of kidney toxicity. Nitrilotriacetic acid is also a recognised carcinogen, and toxic by inhalation and skin contact.

LAUNDRY

Most laundry detergents and powders also contain synthetic fragrance.

Other possible ingredients include bleaches and glycol ethers, which are petroleum derived and are suspected cardiovascular, reproductive, kidney, liver and neurotoxins. Some may be absorbed through the skin, so along with the enzymes (another common ingredient) which break down skin oils and cause skin irritation, you better hope they rinse out well from your clothes! Some laundry detergents contain formaldehyde, a volatile organic compound (VOC) known to be carcinogenic and teratogenic, and which can cause dermatitis,

---

[48] Statham & Schneider, 2012, p.202.

asthma, headaches, and chronic fatigue. Some laundry products also contain nitrilotriacetic acid in Australia, which is banned in the US. Both of these get the double sad face in *The Chemical Maze*. Oh, and yes, you'll find SLES here too, along with accompanying carcinogenic contaminants.

Spot and stain removers often also contain several known carcinogens, and have six common ingredients that get the double sad face.

GENERAL PURPOSE CLEANERS

General purpose cleaners, along with window and glass cleaners, often include ammonia which I am afraid gets the double sad face, and is toxic by skin contact and inhalation, and is suspected of respiratory, liver and neurotoxicity. All purpose cleaners can also contain nitrilotriacetic acid, along with several other sad face chemicals.

DISINFECTANTS & ANTI-BACTERIAL PRODUCTS

No list like this would be complete without disinfectants. How we do so love to disinfect everything these days!

Now you know I am not a purist—I do not advocate becoming obsessed, lest you let all this information overwhelm you. I suggest making gradual changes as you can.

But please, please, stop using any products labelled as antibacterial. It's not that killing bacteria is inherently bad (though it's not inherently good either), it's that many of those antibacterial products are doing two other things that are very bad: they're poisoning you, and they're breeding stronger, super bacteria.

Some of the worst chemicals you might find in disinfectants include triclosan, formaldehyde, phenylphenol, and glutaraldehyde.

Triclosan is closely related to dioxane (see above), and has been found in human breast milk and blood plasma.[49] And triclosan only gets a single sad face in *The Chemical Maze*—the other three chemicals I've listed get the double one! Between them they can cause long term systemic effects including developmental abnormalities, endocrine disruption and reproductive problems, immune system dysfunction, asthma sensitisation and of course, cancer.

'Exposure to this synthetic pesticide [triclosan], which is currently found in the urine of 75 per cent of all people tested, has been linked to cancer, hormone disruption, liver damage, and other health problems.'[50] (Healthychild.org)

In the meantime, the alkalinity of plain soap makes a very good safe disinfectant that is sufficient for most home use—and is now used widely in hospitals as well. White vinegar has been shown to kill 99 per cent of bacteria and 80 per cent of viruses, and several essential oils have also been found to be effective anti-microbials, with evidence to date suggesting bacteria may not develop resistance to

---

[49] Natural Resouces Defense Council, 'Triclosan and Triclocarban', http://www.nrdc.org/living/chemicalindex/triclosan.asp, viewed 7 October 2013.

[50] Alexandra Zissu, 'Skip the Triclosan and Other Antibacterial Products', *Healthy Child Healthy World*, 2013, http://healthychild.org/easy-steps/skip-the-triclosan-and-other-antibacterial-products, viewed 1 October 2013.

them. So if you really do want a good anti-bacterial (say because your family have all had the dreaded gastro), try filling a reusable spray bottle with 500ml (2 cups) white vinegar and adding 5 drops each of lime, tea tree, clove and cinnamon essential oils (just as one example combination). Still, use it sparingly.

Now, after all that, let's finish with some more good news: making your own cleaning products is not only going to be better for your health, it's going to be very much cheaper too. For instance, you might save as much as $40–$80[51] every time you make some homemade laundry detergent (depending how much you make, and what brand you would otherwise buy). That's not bad hey? Check out the next chapter for recipes!

---

[51] 'Rhonda's homemade cleaning products' on *Afternoons with Rebecca*, ABC Brisbane http://blogs.abc.net.au/queensland/2011/10/rhondas-homemade-cleaning-products.html

[10]

Five Non-Toxic Cleaning Recipes to Start You Off

KIRSTEN MCCULLOCH

Kirsten McCulloch is the editor of this book and an Australian writer passionate about living a more sustainable, healthy life—for herself, her family and the planet. She writes about non-toxic cleaning and other aspects of a healthy home at Sustainable Suburbia, *where you can download her free Non-toxic Cleaning Printables.*
http://SustainableSuburbia.net

IN THE INTRODUCTION to this book, I alluded to the fact that we have lost the skills our grandparents had for making their own cleaning products.

Those skills are not altogether forgotten. This chapter will give you a brief run down on how to make some of your own cleaning products, out of basic ingredients like plain soap, vinegar, bicarbonate of soda (baking soda), and lemons.

We'll start with the easiest one over the page.

CITRUS ALL PURPOSE CLEANER

Being an acid, vinegar does a good job cleaning alkaline stains, like rust stains, grass stains, and hard water stains in your toilet or sink. It also kills about 99 per cent of bacteria. D-limonene is a solvent found in all citrus fruit peels, with great grease cutting properties, and that lovely citrus smell. When you soak citrus peel in vinegar, some of the d-limonene infuses the vinegar with extra cleaning power.

YOU WILL NEED

TODAY:

- A wide mouth jar
- Citrus peel
- White vinegar

IN TWO–THREE WEEKS:

- A fine mesh or muslin strainer
- A spray bottle
- Distilled or cool boiled water, or more white vinegar
- Optionally a teaspoon of dishwashing liquid (not soap based)
- Optionally some lime essential oil

INSTRUCTIONS

1. Loosely fill your jar with left over citrus peel of your choice.
2. Fill with vinegar, covering the peel.
3. Leave in a dark place (or at least out of direct sunlight) for two to three weeks.

IN TWO–THREE WEEKS:

1. Strain the vinegar through a fine mesh or muslin strainer. Any pith will block up your spray bottle.

2. You can either use your citrus vinegar neat, dilute it with more vinegar, or dilute it with distilled or boiled water. If you dilute with plain tap water, I recommend only making up enough to use over a week or two, as water is a great bacteria breeding solution.

3. I make up a fairly weak solution (1:4 or even 1:8, depending how much I have), for my kids to clean with, knowing they will spray waaaay more than necessary.

4. Optionally add a few drops of citrus essential oil for extra disinfectant properties and a delightful smell. Lime is my favourite and studies have found it works well against a range of germs.[52] About 30-50 drops per litre of made up spray.

5. Optionally add 1 tsp of your preferred dishwashing liquid (skip this if you make your own soap-based dishwashing liquid). This will give it a little more omph, especially if you skipped the citrus soaking step, however, I usually don't need it.

---

[52] See the next chapter: 'Which Essential Oils Should You Use for Cleaning?'

LAUNDRY POWDER

YOU WILL NEED

- ½–1 cup borax or oxy-bleach[53] (e.g. ecostore's Laundry soaker) (optional)
- 1 cup powdered washing soda (sodium carbonate) (not the crystals, which are hard to mix or dissolve well)
- 2 cups grated soap or soap flakes (about 240g)
- For hard water, add ½ cup citric acid and 2 cups extra washing soda

Note: the only two essential ingredients in this recipe are soap and washing soda.

Mix all ingredients thoroughly, and use 1-2 tablespoons per wash, with an extra tablespoon for hard water. (Note: an Australian tbsp=20ml or 4 metric teaspoons. This varies around the world).

You may need to dissolve your powder first, especially if you are washing in cold water.

Leave out the borax if you are using the grey water on your garden, or for a more eco-friendly mix.

FOR EXTRA HEAVY DUTY POWDER: use a ratio of 1:1:1:1 of the soap, washing soda, borax and oxygen cleaner.

RINSE: Add ¼-½ cup vinegar to the rinse for sensitive skin, or if you notice any soap residue. This also works as a fabric softener.

---

[53] An oxygen bleach is basically sodium percarbonate, and becomes hydrogen peroxide and sodium carbonate (washing soda) when dissolved in water. Some brands contain fillers however, and other chemicals.

LAUNDRY SPOT STAIN REMOVER

In a clean spray bottle, measure in:

- 65 ml (¼ cup) glycerine (buy it in the cleaning section of your supermarket, or from the chemist)
- 65ml (¼ cup) dishwashing liquid (I use ecostore brand)
- 390ml (1½ cups) distilled or cool boiled water

Shake to mix, before each use. Spray on dirty clothes, leave a few minutes and toss in the wash.

This is particularly good on things like tea, coffee, some kinds of ink, juice, sauce and baby spit up—acid and protein based stains, similarly to borax.

Glycerine helps to soften old stains, so if you have an older stain, try spraying it on and leaving for 15-20 minutes before washing, but don't allow it to dry out.

ALTERNATIVE STAIN REMOVERS

You can try just rubbing some dishwashing liquid directly into the stain—particularly good for oil stains—or even just a bar of soap. Or try this:

GENTLE PRE-TREATING SPRAY

- 120 ml (4 fl oz) white vinegar
- 240 ml (8 fl oz) water
- Mix together and pour into a spray bottle. Shake before use.

Uses: spray onto generally grubby clothes before washing, especially onto sweaty areas or grass stains. For extra power use straight vinegar, or on acid and tannin based stains, sprinkle with bicarb soda before spraying.

FOR CLEANING THE BATHROOM

I use my all-purpose citrus spray pretty much everywhere (that is what 'all purpose' means, after all), but sometimes you need a bit more.

DISINFECTANT SPRAY WITH ESSENTIAL OILS

- 30-50 drops essential oils (see below)
- 1 litre vinegar
  Fill a spray bottle with white vinegar. Choose at least 2-3 of the oils listed below. Add 30-50 drops (total) per litre of vinegar. Ideally use at least one oil from the first group.

Studies[54] have found cinnamon, clove, thyme, and lime to be among the most effective disinfectant essential oils, while rosemary, lemon grass, tea tree, peppermint, oregano and other citrus oils are also effective. Clove leaf oil, tea tree oil and vinegar are also effective against mould.

It is impossible to give the oils an exact order of efficacy, since each will be more effective against some pathogens and less against others.

CREAM CLEANSER

If your grubby bath needs a bit more oomph, try this recipe.

---

[54] See Seenivasan Prabuseenivasan et al, 'In vitro antibacterial activity of some plant essential oils', *BMC Complementary and Alternative Medicine* 2006, 6:39, http://www.biomedcentral.com/1472-6882/6/39 and Shigeharu Inouye et al. 'Antibacterial activity of essential oils and their major constituents against respiratory tract pathogens by gaseous contact', *Journal of Antimicrobial Chemotherapy*. (2001) 47 (5): 565-573. http://jac.oxfordjournals.org/content/47/5/565.full

Mix together:

- 1 cup bicarb soda (baking soda)
- ½ cup dishwashing liquid

Mix until you have the consistency of a thick cream cleanser. Depending on the dishwashing liquid you use, you may need to vary the quantities slightly. Keep in mind that bicarb soda is what provides the scrubbing power here, so the more dissolved it is, the less "scrubby" it is, which can be good or bad depending what you are cleaning. For a more abrasive cleaner, add 1 tbsp course salt.

Pour the liquid into a bottle and shake well before use.

If you find you have some white powder residue after cleaning, spray on some vinegar (or the Citrus All Purpose Cleaner) and it will wipe right off, as the vinegar reacts with the soda.

MOULD

Spray with white vinegar and leave for 20 minutes, then wipe off. For stubborn mould, use oil of cloves (clove leaf oil rather than clove bud oil).

Please be aware that essential oils can be toxic if swallowed, and many are contraindicated in certain circumstances, such as pregnancy and for infants. See the cautions in the next chapter for more details.

[11]

Which Essential Oils Should You Use for Cleaning?

KIRSTEN MCCULLOCH

Kirsten McCulloch is the editor of this book and an Australian writer passionate about living a more sustainable, healthy life—for herself, her family and the planet. She writes about non-toxic cleaning and other aspects of a healthy home at Sustainable Suburbia, *where you can download her free Non-toxic Cleaning Printables.*
http://SustainableSuburbia.net

ESSENTIAL OILS CAN enhance your cleaning products by helping them clean, by acting as disinfectants, and of course by creating that lovely 'clean' smell many of us are used to.

Of course, essential oils are also very concentrated and some are safer than others. There are some oils that should not be used during pregnancy or around young children, or only with great care. See the cautions at the end of this chapter for more details, and always keep out of the reach of children.

Here's the low down on seven essential oils to use for good effect.

LIME, ORANGE & THE OTHER CITRUS OILS

The method of soaking citrus peel in vinegar to increase vinegar's cleaning properties works because of the d-limonene in citrus peel, which is an excellent grease cutter. Citrus essential oils likewise contain this cleaning agent. Grapefruit and orange generally have the highest levels of d-limonene, but all citrus fruit have some. They are also effective anti-bacterials. One study, for instance, found that lime oil was one of the most effective antimicrobials of the 21 oils studied, though lemon and orange were not far behind.[55]

I typically use lime oil in my disinfectant cleaning wipes[56] and sometimes add it to my DIY all purpose cleaner.[57] I also use it in my 'faux four thieves' blend that I tend to spray around when there are nasty bugs in the house, as a general anti-microbial. (This is the same as the EO based vinegar disinfectant spray on my non-toxic cleaning printables,[58] only Faux Four Thieves is a much better name, don't you think?)

---

[55] Seenivasan Prabuseenivasan et.al, ' In vitro antibacterial activity of some plant essential oils', *BMC Complementary and Alternative Medicine* 2006, 6:39, http://www.biomedcentral.com/1472-6882/6/39

[56] For instructions on making them see 'DIY Disinfectant Cleaning Wipes' http://sustainablesuburbia.net/diy-disinfectant-cleaning-wipes

[57] See http://sustainablesuburbia.net/how-to-make-citrus-vinegar-spray

[58] Download these at http://sustainablesuburbia.net/non-toxic-printables

EUCALYPTUS OIL

Who doesn't love the smell of eucalyptus oil? Okay, maybe not everyone does, but I do. I use it in my wool wash and often my ordinary laundry liquid too. It's the main reason I like to make the liquid, even though the powder is effective for longer.[59] I just love the smell. Eucalyptus oil is also reputed to have disinfectant properties, and to kill dust mites.

Pure eucalyptus oil (i.e. not the essential oil, though it would probably work too, but at greater cost) makes a good laundry spot stain remover for unknown stains. Pour a few drops onto the stained area and leave for a minute or two. You can also use it to get sticky substances like chewing gum and glue out of clothes, and sticky labels off bottles.

TEA TREE OIL

Tea tree oil is generally considered to be a good anti-bacterial, anti-viral and anti-fungal. I always keep a bottle around as a general antiseptic, and to use as a mosquito repellent. I also use it in my disinfectant cleaning wipes, and it could certainly be used in a four thieves blend. Tea tree oil is also said to be good against mould, but I generally prefer to use clove leaf oil if I have it.

Tea tree oil has been studied relatively extensively, and in particular has been found to be similarly effective against antibiotic resistant strains of bacteria and other strains.

---

[59] See Kirsten McCulloch 'How to Make Laundry Powder or Liquid: The Tutorial and the Science', 2013, http://sustainablesuburbia.net/how-to-make-diy-laundry-powder-or-liquid/

Whether bacteria can also become resistant to tea tree oil is unclear, but the balance of the evidence suggests maybe not—though not all the evidence is in agreement here.[60]

CLOVE OIL

Clove leaf oil (also called oil of cloves) is very effective against mould. Clove bud oil, which is more often found in aromatherapy, is less effective against mould, because it has a lower eugenol content (though presumably it has other benefits when used therapeutically). Clove oil was also found to have the second most effective antimicrobial activity in the study mentioned previously, after cinnamon oil, though it's not clear whether they used leaf or bud oil.[61]

I use clove oil in my faux four thieves spray, and I will use it neat to clean mould, or a little in the washing machine if I have mouldy smelling (but not stained) clothes. But, I find the smell overpowering, so I tend to use it quite sparingly.

CINNAMON OIL

Cinnamon oil gets a mention because it came out as number one in anti-microbial activity, in both the study mentioned previously, and an earlier study which looked at the efficacy of oils in vapour, rather than liquid form.[62]

---

[60] See C. F. Carson et.al, 'Melaleuca alternifolia (Tea Tree) Oil: a Review of Antimicrobial and Other Medicinal Properties' *Clinical Microbiol. Rev.*, January 2006, vol. 19, no. 1, pp 50-62
http://cmr.asm.org/content/19/1/50.full

[61] Seenivasan Prabuseenivasan et.al, 2006 op. cit.

[62] Shigeharu Inouye et al. 'Antibacterial activity of essential oils and their major constituents against respiratory tract pathogens by gaseous

Again, it has quite an overpowering smell (though I personally like it better than the smell of clove oil), so I use it sparingly. It does make it into my four thieves blend though. As an aside wild thyme oil also showed to good effect in that second study, but I really don't like the smell of it, so I mostly use it only in my faux four thieves spray, which I use sparingly as a disinfectant.

ROSEMARY OIL

Rosemary also has antimicrobial properties, and as a bonus is often a good remedy for headaches, plus it has that invigorating scent that you probably need if you're busy cleaning, right?

I mostly keep rosemary around for when I have a cold and I add it to my shower disks,[63] but you can also use it in your cleaning products for a lovely refreshing scent. Try cleaning your kitchen floor with a bucket of water to which you've added ¼ cup vinegar and 5-10 drops of rosemary oil.

PEPPERMINT OIL

Peppermint oil had similar microbial efficacy to lemon and orange oil in the first study mentioned above. It also did reasonably well in the second study, though it wasn't a patch on cinnamon, lemongrass or thyme.

---

contact', *Journal of Antimicrobial Chemotherapy*, 2001, 47 (5): 565-573. http://jac.oxfordjournals.org/content/47/5/565.full

[63] See http://sustainablesuburbia.net/diy-cold-flu-remedies-for-those-end-of-season-bugs-shower-disks-vapor-rub

I always keep peppermint oil around for my cold & flu remedies, but it can be also used in cleaning. It's also said to be a pest repellent, particularly for mice.

SAFETY & CAUTIONS:

Always keep your essential oils out of the reach of children. Ingesting a couple of tablespoons of some oils could be fatal. Generally, don't use any oils on young children's skin, and especially keep the eucalyptus and peppermint away from their faces, as they can cause some children to have difficulty breathing. There have been documented cases of death in infants who have had peppermint oil applied around their nostrils.[64] Essential oils should also be used with caution by pregnant women: most oils are okay to use in a vapouriser, but not necessarily on your skin, so use gloves when cleaning with essential oils. In particular, rosemary and peppermint should generally be avoided in pregnancy.

For more information on essential oil safety, the booklet *Using Essential Oils Safely* by Lea Harris is a good resource.[65]

WHICH BRAND OF ESSENTIAL OIL SHOULD YOU USE?

Okay, firstly, let's dispel a few myths.

---

[64] See Katharine Koeppen, 'Adverse Reactions to Peppermint Oil'. http://www.aromaceuticals.com/blog/adverse-reactions-to-peppermint-oil, viewed 25 October 2013.

[65] Download it from *Learning About EOs* http://www.learningabouteos.com/

1. While price is relevant, an oil that costs a whole lot more is by no means necessarily a better oil. On the other hand, I personally tend to avoid brands that are significantly cheaper than the ones I find in my health food store, since substitution of cheaper oil components and 'nature identical' synthetics can occur.

2. Any oil brand that tells you it's certified therapeutic is certified by itself. In other words, that is just marketing mumbo jumbo. Oils can be certified organic (look for a certifying body), and in Australia they can be listed with the Therapeutic Goods Association (TGA), which means they must be manufactured by someone holding a certification of Good Manufacturing Practice, but not that they have been tested by the TGA. Some essential oils may need to be *registered* with the TGA which involves more checks than listing, but, most are simply listed. However, registration costs a packet, and smaller companies generally won't have it. That doesn't necessarily mean they are shonky (it does mean they can't legally make therapeutic claims for their oils in Australia—they can still sell them though).

3. All essential oils are pure oils, so telling you it's pure is, again, just marketing hype. After all, they're hardly going to admit it's not pure are they? That would be the same as saying it wasn't actually an essential oil.

OTHER USEFUL CONSIDERATIONS

1. For aromatherapy purposes you want a quality oil, and it makes a difference where the plant was grown. So if the brand of oil you are looking at doesn't tell you where the oil came from (eg Tasmanian Lavender vs Bulgarian), it mostly likely means it is just an amalgam, which means the outcomes are less predictable. This is certainly a quality signal, but on the other hand, if you are not a qualified aromatherapist, you won't know whether you want Tasmanian or Bulgarian lavender anyway.

2. Another quality signal is the inclusion of the latin name of the plant on the label (since there are sometimes more than one plant with the same common name, e.g. Lavender which can be *Lavandula angustifolia* or *Lavandula latifolia*, also known as Spike Lavender), and where applicable the chemotype.⁶⁶ Only some oils have multiple chemotypes, indicated by the letters ct. before the type. For example, Rosemary has three chemotypes, camphor, verbenone, and 1,8-cineole.

3. If you want to, you should be able to get GC/MS (Gas chromatography–mass spectrometry) test results from your company of choice, for any given oil. There are a limited number of large oil distillers in the world, and most companies get their oil through them. But, if they care about quality, they will be test-

---

⁶⁶ Different chemotypes occur when one plant species has adapted in different ways, typically in different locations, to have a reliably different chemical composition to the original plant.

ing them before they package them for you. (I don't expect you to know how to read the test results, but if you can get them, that's a good sign.)

4. For cleaning purposes, I simply don't worry too much. Because I'm in Australia I generally buy a TGA listed brand, and leave it at that.

5. If you are in the US, you might find a mini study interesting, in which several brands of tea tree oil were tested by an independent lab (they've also tested myrrh and peppermint oil). Most were found to be 'compliant' with the norm for tea tree oil, including some brands that are relatively inexpensive.[67]

---

[67] Lea Harris, '3rd Party Testing on 10 different brands of Tea Tree Essential' see
http://www.learningabouteos.com/index.php/2013/08/10/3rd-party-test-results-master-list/

FOOD
& WATER

[12]

Surely Food's Not Toxic?

KIRSTEN MCCULLOCH

Kirsten McCulloch is the editor of this book and an Australian writer passionate about living a more sustainable, healthy life—for herself, her family and the planet. She writes about non-toxic cleaning and other aspects of a healthy home at Sustainable Suburbia, where you can download her free Non-toxic Cleaning Printables.
http://SustainableSuburbia.net

WHEN WE TALK about the toxic chemicals in our food, most people will think of the pesticides and herbicides with which they are often sprayed and grown.

But did you know that there are about 350 approved food additives which may also be in much of the food you eat?[68] And that's not including the thousands of 'flavours' that don't need to be named individually, as they are

---

[68] Food Intolerance Network factsheet: 'Complete List of Additives', http://fedup.com.au/information/information/complete-lists-of-additives, viewed 10 October 2013.

considered to be trade secrets. Of course most additives are generally safe—as far as we know.

However, 50 of those everyday food additives are likely to cause problems for some people.[69] And worse, most people are unaware they are affected.

Sue Dengate's book *Fed Up: Understanding how food affects your child and what you can do about it* is filled with stories of people who've spent their entire lives affected by food additives or natural food chemicals in various ways—anything from asthma to allergies to 'brain fog' to ADHD—only to discover in their twenties or thirties or later, that cutting out certain food chemicals could make a dramatic change in their lives. There are also, of course, many cases of parents desperate to find a way of helping their children, again with both physical and behavioural issues.

'He's like a different child,' Sarah told me of her six-year-old son, William.[70] 'Before we started the diet, he was borderline ODD [oppositional defiance disorder]. He still has some difficulties, especially with reading other kids' body language and faces, but he's much better overall. If he has certain food additives though, he gets really aggressive.'

Sarah put her whole family on the 'Failsafe' exclusion diet, cutting out not only artificial food additives, but also certain natural food chemicals, to find out what they reacted to. What she discovered was that she, as well as her son, felt much better without certain foods in her diet.

---

[69] Ibid.
[70] Names have been changed to protect privacy.

As well as affecting her son's behaviour, some foods affect them physically, she explained. 'We've been doing it long enough now that I can predict certain things,' she said, 'like if William has some orange at school, and then we have sweet potato at dinner, he will wet the bed that night, every time.'

But how do food additives affect 'ordinary' children and their families?

There have been a few small and larger experiments done in schools around the world, testing to see whether removing food additives from children's diets would make a difference to their behaviour and learning abilities.

One study done in New York covered an entire school district, with 803 schools.[71] Additives were gradually removed from free school lunches and breakfasts, over a four year period. By the end of that time, school rankings for the area had risen from 5 per cent below the national average to 11 per cent above it, and 75,000 children were no longer classified as learning disabled. No other school district reported such a large gain. Nor was the gain all due to a single change. Rather there were three diet changes over the period,

---

[71] See Schoenthaler, SJ, Doraz WE, Wakefield JA. 1986 – The Impact of a Low Food Additive and Sucrose Diet on Academic Performance in 803 New York City Public Schools, International Journal of Biosocial Research, Vol. 8(2): 185-195 and

Schoenthaler, SJ, Doraz WE, Wakefield JA. 1986a – The Testing of Various Hypotheses as Explanations for the Gains in National Standardized Academic Test Scores in the 1978-1983 New York City Nutrition Policy Modification Project, International Journal of Biosocial Research, Vol. 8(2): 196-203

and each time more additives were removed, there was a significant jump in scores.[72]

With more immediate effects, a class of 6 year olds in the UK was asked to avoid additives for two weeks in 2003. The result?

'[N]early 60 per cent of parents reported an improvement in their child's behaviour, sleep patterns and cooperation.'[73]

Similar results have been found in other schools in both the UK and Australia, with parents, children and teachers reporting improvements.

So how can you figure out if you, or your children, are sensitive to food additives? The standard method is to undergo an elimination diet, where you remove food additives, and in some cases foods naturally high in certain food chemicals, and then gradually reintroduce them in the form of 'challenges'. The Failsafe diet, recommended by the Food Intolerance Network, is based on an elimination diet developed by doctors at the Royal Prince Alfred Hospital Allergy Unit in Sydney, Australia. You can find more information on the Food Intolerance Network's website, www.fedup.com.au, or in Sue Dengate's books *Fed Up:*

---

[72] For more information see Food Intolerance Network factsheet 'New York City Public Schools: Four Years of Success', http://fedup.com.au/factsheets/support-factsheets/school-factsheets, viewed 18 September, 2013

[73] Food Intolerance Network factsheet 'Schools: Eating for Success', http://fedup.com.au/factsheets/support-factsheets/schools-eating-for-success, viewed 11 October 2013.

Understanding how food affects your child and what you can do about it, and *The Failsafe Cookbook.*

Read the next chapter for an introduction to an elimination diet, but note that it only covers more commonly known food intolerances such as dairy and gluten intolerance, and does not look at food additives.

[13]

Allergy and Intolerance Elimination Diet

DR. TERAY GARCHITORENA KUNISHI

Dr. Teray Garchitorena Kunishi, ND is co-founder of the Berkeley Naturopathic Medical Group in Berkeley, California. Her workshops and programs provide solutions for depression, anxiety, fatigue, chronic stress and insomnia, ADHD and PTSD.
http://www.berkeleynaturopathic.com

FINDING AND AVOIDING your food sensitivities is one of the most important keys to avoiding medication and healing naturally from chronic health issues. It takes a good bit of commitment and effort, but the potential benefits—more energy, less allergies, clearer skin, sharper mind—are well worth it!

The basic technique is to temporarily remove common allergens from the diet:

1. Gluten
2. Dairy

3. Sugar
4. Eggs
5. Peanuts
6. Any known or suspected allergens.

Gluten is a protein found in wheat, barley, rye, kamut, spelt and faro. Some examples of gluten free grains are: rice, quinoa, millet and buckwheat. Oats are technically gluten-free, but are often contaminated with gluten.

Dairy includes yogurt, whey, milk, cheese and butter.

The best way to go about this is to first observe which meals you eat containing any of these foods. You may be dismayed to find that breakfast, lunch and dinner are choc-full of these potential offenders, but take heart. There are lots of cookbooks that have wonderful recipes that exclude common allergens.

You'll need to read labels because these foods find their way into many packaged products. The easiest way to avoid these foods is to avoid processed foods altogether.

Next, try out some recipes and begin to plot out your strategy for the detox/elimination diet. Think about what snacks to keep on hand so that you don't give in to the temptation to grab a pastry or a milkshake on your way to work.

Write down all your current symptoms and how bad they are on a scale of one to five. That way you can refer to it at the end of your detox to see what changed.

For example: *Headaches—3/5, daily. Runny nose, 2/5, worse when outdoors.*

When you're ready, start your detox diet. Make sure *not* to restrict portions—this is not about losing weight! Eat as much as you need to feel satisfied. Expect to have a few rough days until cravings for your favorite foods subside. Drink lots of water and plan on resting as much as possible.

After 2-4 weeks, note how you feel. Review your list of symptoms and see if anything has changed. Most people feel lighter, clearer and have less severe symptoms.

Then, re-introduce each food group, one at a time, every three days. Make sure to eat a few servings of the food— for example, several pieces of bread and a serving of pasta when you challenge wheat. This way, you'll provoke a strong reaction. If you feel worse, you'll know which foods are responsible.

Good luck and have fun with this very illuminating adventure!

Note: This detox diet is not right for everyone! Always talk to your health professional before making changes to your diet, exercise or medications.

[14]

Organic Versus Conventional Food: What's the Real Price?

JOANNA COZENS

Joanna Cozens is one half of the duo behind www.dailyorganic.com.au, a site dedicated to discovering, sharing and inspiring more Australians to live organically, sustainably, ethically one step, one banana, one cleaning product at a time.
http://www.dailyorganic.com.au

I'M GOING TO play Devil's advocate for a sec. Here's the thing: a lot of people think buying organic food is expensive. Now, I'd like to say that's not true but, to call a spade a spade, I'd be lying. In fact, a recent study by Suncorp Bank shows there's an average 79 per cent difference in price between organic and conventional produce. Despite this, some research predicts organics will be one of Australia's top five growth industries in 2013. Geez, is anybody else's head spinning yet? And it's only the first paragraph!

Deep breath. Okay. Buying organic food generally means you're paying a fair price to farmers who are doing the right thing by the environment and their animals. Then again, it's hard to argue with the lure of non-organic milk that only costs a dollar a litre. On the down-down-prices-are-down side, we all know that paying such a small amount for our milk means the farmer isn't getting a fair go—and it's destroying their livelihoods and families.

Also, some people say it's impossible to feed a family three square meals if you feed them only organic food—and, really, who can't sympathise with that? But, in actuality, the average Australian household spends more on junk food and alcohol than fruit and vegetables. As a result, we also spend more on medical bills, so it's not exactly a good long-term plan, despite being cheaper on shopping day.

I could go on but the point of this article is not to change the world (not today anyway, give me 'til next week at least!), it's to show that, all arguments aside, you can strike a balance between health and ethical concerns AND your purse strings. So, here are some tips for saving money while getting better quality eating into your life.

THE CLEAN 15 AND THE DIRTY DOZEN

No, it's not a movie starring Clint Eastwood. The Clean 15 and The Dirty Dozen are your tickets to spending your organic dollars more wisely. Because not all conventional foods are pesticide laden and, if your budget doesn't stretch to a purely organic lifestyle, you have options. Based on the results of almost 43,000 tests conducted by America's Environmental Working Group, it was estimated that consumers could reduce their pesticide exposure by almost 90 per cent if they avoided the most contaminated foods and ate the least contaminated foods instead. So, The Clean 15 (aka the guy in the white hat) is a list of 15 fruits and vegies that are relatively pesticide-free, and The Dirty Dozen (aka the guy in the black hat) is a list of fruits and vegies that can expose you to about 15 different pesticides each day.

In alphabetical order, here's The Clean 15:

asparagus
avocado
cabbage
corn
eggplant
grapefruit
kiwifruit
mangoes
mushrooms
onions
pineapples
rockmelon
snow peas
sweet potatoes
watermelon

And here's The Dirty Dozen:

apples
blueberries
capsicum
celery
cucumbers

grapes
lettuce
nectarines
peaches
potatoes
spinach
strawberries[75]

JOIN A FOOD CO-OP

I can't begin to tell you (although, technically, I suppose I just did) how much I love cracking the lid on a box of fresh, organic fruit and vegies from my local food co-op. I never know exactly what I'll get—and that's half the fun! All I know for sure is it's great seasonal produce, it's fresh and it's local, which means it's spent less time in storage and therefore tastes great. It also means I get terrific discounts and the convenience of not having to leave the house to shop.

CUT DOWN ON MEAT

Okay, okay, you will generally pay more for meat that's raised in an organic or sustainable manner. But the up side is that you know it's been produced ethically and, to many

---

[75] Editor's note: In 2012 Friends of the Earth released a report called "The Dose Makes the Poison?" Their list of the 20 Australian foods with the most pesticide levels detected in 2010-2011 was, in order, apples, wheat, strawberries, pears, grapes, lettuce, nectarines, peaches, bread, bran biscuits, tea (imported), barley, tomatoes, apricots, canola, flour, carrots, plums, green beans. They note that the results should be taken as indicative only. See the full report at http://www.foe.org.au/sites/default/files/TheDoseMakesThePoisonFeb2012_0.pdf

of us, that matters more than a bargain. We've all seen the pictures of battery hens and over-crowded piggeries and it breaks our hearts. So now Dave and I pay a little more for our meat but we eat less of it and we get creative with some of the less popular cuts.

PLAN AHEAD

Create your meal plans ahead of time. That way you buy what you want, when you want it, and you don't stock your fridge and cupboards up with stuff that will go to waste.

BUY SEASONAL

This is a no-brainer, really. It costs less to buy your fruit and vegies if they're in season. They taste better, too, especially (particularly) if they're bought from local suppliers. Which brings us to...

BUY LOCAL

One of the big benefits of buying local is the environmental savings. In other words, the amount of petrol it takes to get a local tomato from the farm and into your mouth is way less than one that's been shipped in from overseas.

BUY DIRECT FROM THE FARM

For a fixed price, a local farmer can deliver a box of fresh food to your door every week. Not only does this guarantee you'll be eating the freshest organic food possible, you'll also be helping out the farmer.

BUY IN BULK

Offer to buy a crate of produce from a farmer (rather than just a couple of spuds) and you're guaranteed to get a better price. If you've got room in your freezer, you can also do the same with organic meat. So get together with your friends and see what you can come up with. The more the merrier—and cheaper! Also, if your local market or organic food shop sells stuff in bulk bins, you're bound to get a great deal there, too.

GET YOUR GREEN THUMB ON!

You don't need ten acres, a tractor and a flannelette shirt to grow your own food. Get yourself one of those long pots and you've enough space to grow fresh herbs or mixed salad greens that you can pick as needed. Tomatoes don't need much space either. There are even varieties that can be trained up your walls. Passionfruit, too, grows like the clappers, keeps you in fruit for years and covers up an unsightly wall to boot. The sky's the limit, folks!

[15]

The Inconvenient Truth About Most Convenience Foods

ALEXX STUART

Alexx Stuart is on a mission to help people eat better and be more conscious of what we use on our skin and in our homes, while eradicating guilt and feelings of deprivation. Her first book Real Treats *shot to #1 Amazon best seller within 12 hours of publishing. Alexx is also available for speaking engagements, workshops and commissioned articles. http://alexxstuart.com*

THERE'S AN INCONVENIENT truth about most convenience foods. It's that convenient often means the cost is elsewhere or down the line as Prince Charles, staunch slow food and ethical food advocate, said in a wonderful speech earlier this year.[76] Sometimes the convenience is

---

[76] Prince Charles Spoke at the Langendurg Forum 2013 in Germany. See 'We are not amused: Prince launches scathing attack on food

packaged as time, and sometimes as money.

Take a look at this convenience item I found in the super market as the perfect example to illustrate this point—this one packaged as a time saver. I'm excluding brand as this is not about defaming, so much as raising consciousness. If we use harsher criteria overall, it won't matter about knowing what brands to buy or not buy. With a quick scan of the eye, we'll know in a blink whether the convenience is worth it or not, and many more people will make more leaps over to produce, from packet land.

It's 125g of chicken breast, sliced and ready to go for a salad topper, sandwich or stir fry. I laughed with the 'handy resealable pouch' claim. It's supposedly 2.5 servings—I suppose that's to get you needing to snack all afternoon on more convenience foods to spend more money, because 50g of chicken sure ain't much chicken.

NUTRITION INFORMATION

Servings per package: Approx 2.5
Average Serving Size: 50g

Ingredients: Chicken Breast (98%), Maize Starch, Salt, Vegetable Gum (Carrageenan), Citrus, Flour, White Pepper.

Made from local & imported ingredients.

LET'S LOOK AT HOW IT COSTS US FINANCIALLY.

$5.41 for 125g of non organic chicken. That's a whopping $43.28 per kilo. One could buy 2 huge organic chickens for that price totalling about 4kg. No hormones, no GMO seed feeds. Free roaming. There's zero cost convenience at all

---

industry', http://www.foodnavigator.com/Financial-Industry/We-are-not-amused-Prince-launches-scathing-attack-on-food-industry

when you compare the kilo price. A 125g portion of organic chicken from home roasted chook, would be $1.90. So while one might be thinking, 'oh that's good, a $5 lunch option with a couple of crackers and tomato', it turns out to be quite expensive compared to what you could have prepared with nothing but a little forward planning, while making something else. Roast two chooks at once. I've got a delicious recipe on my site.[77] One for eating with the family on the night, and the other for cutting up and freezing for future grab and go meals. Zero additives and organic *and* in this case being a massive saving per serve.

LET'S NOW LOOK AT THE HEALTH COST OF THIS CONVENIENCE

The ingredients: 98 per cent chicken with added Maize starch (corn), salt, carrageenan, citrus, flour, white pepper

MAIZE STARCH: for our GMO (genetically modified organism) clue there's a corn ingredient and the product doesn't specify GM free anywhere *and* it's made from local and imported ingredients. So, I'm guessing that maize starch is hot off the fields of a GM corn farm in the States, sadly, as 90 per cent of corn is GM in the States and makes its way into many packaged food recipes for its low cost and textural enhancement of foods.

SALT: Man-made salt has 3 minerals. Real salt has over 50 minerals. Minerals have gone walk-about in our modern Western diet with artificially fertilised soil, fake salt and

---

[77] See Alexx Stuart 'Roast Chicken – Yes you can!', http://alexxstuart.com/roast-chicken

processed diet choices, and any opportunity you have to add natural minerals back in: Take it! Magnesium deficiency for example, can manifest with symptoms like spasms, cramps, tics, insomnia, chronic fatigue, migraine, IBS, anxiety... *The Magnesium Miracle* is a sensational book if you fancy delving into this subject a little more.

CARRAGEENAN: A proven inflammatory stabiliser used in packaged foods which the *Healthy Home Economist* fills you in on.[78]

FLOUR: Hope no one with gluten intolerance missed that on the label.

While these ingredients only make up 2 per cent of the total product, I take the stance that there's no minimum safety on toxic stuff and if we say to ourselves 'oh, it's only just a little bit toxic' then what are we saying about our self respect? You are WORTH natural, beautiful ingredients. 100 per cent. Your current and future health is worth 100 per cent natural, beautiful ingredients.

LET'S LOOK AT OTHER COSTS

The ethics of feeding chickens on possible GM grains, possible excess antibiotics and not pasture raising them.

The consequence of buying food packaged in a massive plastic pouch relative to the size of the portion, and how much more plastic is used per chicken—about 10 pouches—relative to its weight, instead of perhaps 1 plastic sleeve over

---

[78] See Sarah Pope, 'The Ingredient Allowed in Organic Food that Can Cause Cancer', 2012, http://www.thehealthyhomeeconomist.com/the-ingredient-allowed-in-organic-food-that-can-cause-cancer

a whole chook, or even none, if buying fresh from your ethical butcher.

The consequence of the BPA in the ink dyes used to colour that pouch.

The consequence of the food miles of shipping all those plastic pouches around to supermarkets nationally.

Our ability to make a difference is in every food decision for our health, for animals we choose to eat/not to eat, and the health of the planet. We are in control and we can make a difference. I've no doubt most of you who read this are already actively shaping the world with your shopping baskets, but I still find now I can get better and better at doing it even after years of shopping better, so please share if you think this simple example might help someone shop more consciously.

They really try and frame it so well to make us buy stuff, and that's fine if it's a good thing that's good for us and good for the planet, but when it's not, I just LOVE making an example of them and helping more people see that we're a real voice, here. They won't make stuff if it doesn't sell. It's that simple. If we stop buying the bad stuff that's over packaged, with additives and unethical meat, then they'll stop making it. Job done and when that day comes, we'll be able to say WE DID THAT.

The cost of Real Food is often far far less expensive, especially when we look at the big picture.

What do you think? Seen anything lately that's made you go all detective on it? Warning. Food 'detectivism' is addictive. Trust me, I'm a lifer.

Five Foods That Have Sneaky Additives

SONIA DONALDSON

Natural New Age Mum is a little part of the internet where Aussie mum of two, Sonia Donaldson, shares her tips on living a happy, healthy, holistic lifestyle. The blog features topics on healthy whole food, living chemical free, saving the environment and inspiration for the soul.
http://www.naturalnewagemum.com

DON'T YOU HATE it when you think you are eating something healthy and then someone tells you it's not so healthy?

That's exactly how I felt when I found out about these five foods.

You really have to read labels, ask questions and educate yourself about what is in your food.

This is even more important if your family is having health issues, allergies or reactions to additives.

Here are five foods that would seem healthy, but unfortunately, they can all contain sneaky additives!

1. PRAWNS

Prawns can contain 223 or sodium metabisulphite. Sue Dengate at her website, *Fed Up* says

> 'Prawns always contain sulphites to preserve colour. The maximum permitted level is 30 ppm, but how well is it monitored? One seafood worker explained how they use 'metta' (sodium metabisulphite, 223). It is a white powder sprinkled over sackfuls of fresh prawns by people wearing rubber gloves. Some prawns must have higher readings than others.'[79]

2. GRATED CHEESE

Check on the back of your grated cheese. Quite often it will contain anti-caking agent 460.

It is also called 'cellulose microcrystalline and powdered'—it's essentially wood pulp! Although *Additive Alert* tells us it is 'generally regarded as safe' it has been banned in UK baby food.[80] 'Cellulose is non soluble, but can be fermented in the large intestine. Large concentrations can cause intestinal problems, such as bloating, constipation

---

[79] Food Intolerance Network Factsheet: 'Sulphites (220-228)' http://fedup.com.au/factsheets/additive-and-natural-chemical-factsheets/220-228-sulphite-preservatives

[80] Additive Alert 'Search Additives: 460' http://www.additivealert.com.au/search.php

and diarrhoea.'[81] Not something I really want to eat, thanks all the same!

3. VEGEMITE

I can already hear you all saying, but it's a health food! I found this one out many years ago and banished Vegemite from our house!

Sue Dengate at *Fed Up* says that 'yeast extracts contain free glutamates that are essentially the same as MSG'.[82] Vegemite also contains natural colour (150d) which contains preservative 220. I have talked about 220 on my blog.[83] Tanya at *Additive Free Pantry* has talked about why she gave up vegemite.[84]

4. MILK

Milk is milk is milk.....right? Not so! Read the label to make sure you are getting 100 per cent milk! Choice Australia says 'more than a third of branded 'milk' products contain non-dairy additives, such as minerals, vitamins, or vegetable or fish oil. Under the Food Standards Code the manufacturers

---

[81] 'Vegetable Gums, Emulsifiers, Stabilisers Etc.'
http://mbm.net.au/health/400-495.htm

[82] Food Intolerance Network Factsheet: 'MSG, MSG boosters, flavour enhancers and natural glutamates'
http://fedup.com.au/factsheets/additive-and-natural-chemical-factsheets/621-msg-and-the-new-flavour-enhancers

[83] Sonia Donaldson 'Is Your Dried Fruit Safe?' Natural New Age Mum
http://naturalnewagemum.com/is-your-dried-fruit-safe

[84] Tanya Winfield 'MSG in a Jar' Additive Pantry
http://additivefreepantry.com/index.php?option=com_content&view=article&id=49:msg-in-a-jar&catid=8:blog&Itemid=131

are not allowed to call these products 'milk' on the label, yet they look like milk, are packaged like milk and are kept in the milk fridge in the supermarket.'[85]

5. VITAMINS

Okay so not really a 'food', but still something we give to our kids to ingest. The very things you buy to improve your health may actually be damaging it. Kids' vitamins can contain artificial colours, flavours and additives. One brand for example will tell you that it contains artificial flavours and hydrogenated soy bean oil (what's the bet that isn't GMO free!), among other things.

INGREDIENTS: Granulated Calcium Carbonate (Calcium Carbonate, Dextrose Monohydrate, Sugar, Microcrystalline Cellulose, Maltodextrin), Sorbitol, Sodium Ascorbate, Ferrous Fumarate, Natural and Artificial Flavors, Hydrogenated Soybean Oil, Pregelatinized Starch, Gelatin, Vitamin E Acetate, Stearic Acid, Corn Starch; Less Than 2% Of: Aspartame†, Beta-Carotene, Biotin, Calcium Pantothenate, Cupric Oxide, FD&C Blue #2 Aluminum Lake, FD&C Red #40 Aluminum Lake, FD&C Yellow #6 Aluminum Lake, Folic Acid, Magnesium Stearate, Niacinamide, Potassium Iodide, Pyridoxine Hydrochloride, Riboflavin, Silicon Dioxide, Thiamine Mononitrate, Vitamin A Acetate, Vitamin B_{12}, Vitamin D_3 (Cholecalciferol), Zinc Oxide.

Contains: Tree Nuts (Coconut), Soy.

†PHENYLKETONURICS: CONTAINS PHENYLALANINE

KEEP OUT OF REACH OF CHILDREN

---

[85] 'Milk Products Review' Choice Australia http://www.choice.com.au/reviews-and-tests/food-and-health/food-and-drink/beverages/milk-products-compared-2009/page/non-dairy-additives.aspx

Sooooo I don't want to freak you all out! I just want you to know this information and be aware. It doesn't mean you have to stop eating them. It means you now have the information to make a choice. You might like to change brands or grate your own cheese for example. *Knowledge is power!*

[17]

Are Water Filters Justified?

NICOLE BIJLSMA

Nicole Bijlsma is a building biologist, author of the best seller—Healthy Home, Healthy Family and CEO of the Australian College of Environmental Studies. She has featured on every major Australian television network and lectures and writes about the health hazards in the home.
http://www.buildingbiology.com.au

LIKE AIR, DRINKING water quality is something most of us take for granted, but can we afford to be so complacent? Australians often brag that they have one of the cleanest drinking water supplies in the world. Theoretically this assumption is correct if you drink it from the protected forest catchment areas. As this is not permitted, the chemicals that are consequently added to 'purify' the water and the hundreds of kilometres of pipes through which it must travel, affect the quality of water that ultimately comes out of your tap.

Bottle-fed babies and young children are particularly susceptible to the contaminants likely to be in their drinking water as they drink up to four times more water for their body weight than most adults. The source of your drinking water will determine the type of contaminants that are likely to be present and consequently the ideal water filtration system you should consider. For a discussion on the various contaminants present in tap, tank, bore/well and bottled water, refer to my book: *Healthy Home, Healthy Family*.

WHICH TYPE OF WATER FILTER?

I am often asked, 'What's the best water filter to buy?' and there is no simple answer to this question. This will depend on:

1. How much money you are willing to spend.
2. What contaminants you wish to remove which will largely depend on your source of drinking water: tap, tank or bore/well. The ideal filtration system for each of these sources is discussed in my book *Healthy Home, Healthy Family*.[86]
3. Whether you want a portable system (if you are renting or have a budget) versus a plumbed-in system.
4. How much bench space you have.
5. Your water pressure; the more units incorporated into your water filtration system, the more pressure you will require.

---

[86] http://www.buildingbiology.com.au/index.php/Books/Healthy-Home-Healthy-Family/flypage.tpl.html

6. Whether you want a *point of use (POU) system* ie one that is located at the kitchen tap or shower OR a *point of entry (POE) system*. Whole house systems are installed at your water meter and filter all the water coming into your home. Be mindful however that apart from their expense, these systems will not remove contaminants arising from your domestic plumbing.

> *½ kg of activated carbon has a surface area of between 60 to 150 acres*

TYPES OF WATER FILTERS FOR HOME USE

Water filtration is a basic science—each type of filter media will be unique in its ability to remove certain contaminants—so don't be fooled by companies making outrageous claims about their products for which there is little evidence. Water filtration systems will generally consist of one or more of the following:

SEDIMENT FILTERS are designed to remove particles such as dirt, rust, sand and clay and to protect carbon filters from clogging up too quickly. They can be made from a variety of different materials including polypropylene, polyester, cotton, cellulose, ceramic, wound string and glass fibre and come in a variety of micron sizes—1, 5 and 10 microns. The smaller the size, the more effective they are at trapping smaller particles.

CARBON FILTERS are sourced from organic matter such as wood, coal, bamboo, or coconut which are exposed to high temperatures in an oxygen deprived environment.

They are then 'activated' to increase their ability to adsorb contaminants by heating them with oxidising gas or other chemicals to break them into a fine powder. Apart from improving the taste, colour and odour of the water, carbon filters will effectively remove sediment, pesticides, petrochemicals, chlorine and its carcinogenic by-products (trihalomethanes). However they will only partially remove fluoride and heavy metals such as copper and lead. Their efficiency at removing contaminants will vary depending upon their micron size (0.5, 1, 5 and 10 microns), how effectively they are activated, and what they are derived from. In addition, their effectiveness declines rapidly with use as the absorption sites get used. If you wish to remove heavy metals, use a carbon filter impregnated with KDF. These filters need to be replaced *before* the manufacturer's use-by-date as the effective life of a carbon filter is difficult to establish and bacteria will grow on the filter media.

CERAMIC FILTERS are cheap, long lasting and portable filters that effectively remove bacteria, chlorine, sediment and rust. However ceramic filters are not effective in removing heavy metals or pesticides, require regular maintenance (scrubbing to remove the biofilm), are slow to filter and can quickly clog up. Most ceramic filters consequently come with a carbon cartridge to remove organic contaminants such as pesticides and petrochemicals.

ION EXCHANGE RESIN FILTERS are used to remove heavy metals, fluoride and nitrates and to soften hard water. Whilst a variety of resins have been used including aluminosilicates, heavy metals, and synthetic resins like acrylic, the most widely used resin is styrene-DVB (divinylbenzene) gel polymer. However they do not remove sediment, pesticides, microbes or chlorine. Furthermore bacteria may grow on the resins and they may leak tiny resin fragments into the water supply which is why I don't recommend them.

KDF FILTERS consist of copper and zinc granules using an oxidation/reduction reaction to remove a wide range of contaminants including *free chlorine, heavy metals and iron,* as well as bacteria, algae and fungi. However it does not remove organic chemicals (pesticides, disinfection by products such as THMs) or parasitic cysts, and it can release contaminants back into the water once the filter becomes clogged. In addition they need to be periodically backwashed with hot water to remove the insoluble contaminants. Consequently KDF filters are not commonly used in household systems unless they are combined with a carbon filter.

UV STERILISERS are commonly used in aquariums and to sterilise medical equipment because they kill bacteria, algae and parasites and reduce cysts. They are not commonly used for water filtration in homes that rely on tap water as chlorinated water will effectively kill bacteria in the distribution system. However they should be considered as an additional add-on to a reverse osmosis system if you are ingesting tank water.

REVERSE OSMOSIS FILTERS are a multi-stage system incorporating various sediment and carbon filters as well as a semi-permeable membrane. This system will effectively remove fluoride, pesticides, petrochemicals, chlorine and its by-products, asbestos, nitrates, radium and heavy metals (lead, copper, cadmium, chromium aluminium...). However they are expensive to buy, install and maintain, they will need to be plumbed in and they expend a considerable amount of waste water which will need to be diverted. Furthermore they require considerable under sink bench space. There is a concern that reverse osmosis water is 'dead and acidic' water. However most water found in lakes and rivers is slightly acidic (it absorbs carbon dioxide in the air to form carboxylic acid). As for the absence of minerals, my argument is that you shouldn't be relying on water for this anyway. In response, many people alkalise their RO water which I do not recommend.

> SHOULD I DRINK ALKALINE WATER?
>
> *There is insufficient evidence to validate the claim that drinking alkaline water leads to alkaline blood—indeed a narrow change in blood pH would result in death! Similarly drinking excessive amounts of alkaline water may affect stomach acidity and interfere with protein digestion amongst other issues.*

An economical solution for most families who cannot afford a Reverse Osmosis system will be to purchase a twin or triple stage portable or undersink system featuring a *1.0 micron pleated sediment filter* along with one or two *0.5 micron activated carbon block filters*. However if finances are an issue, a single stage system incorporating one dual function cartridge featuring a sediment filter and a 1 micron (or less) carbon block filter will still be of benefit.

[18]

A Close Brush with Poison —So What's Wrong with Fluoride, Really?

DR SARAH LANTZ

Dr Sarah Lantz (PhD) is a researcher, writer and mother. She has a background in public and population health and is the author of the bestselling book, Chemical Free Kids: Raising Healthy Children in a Toxic World. *She is currently a Research Fellow at the University of Queensland.*
http://www.chemicalfreekids.com.au

FLUORIDE IS ONE of those issues that runs deep with people—like vaccination, religion and money. Those in favour argue that its addition to public water supplies and toothpastes has been a boon to dental health, providing a cost-effective and equitable way to prevent tooth decay. Opponents argue that evidence for its safety and efficacy is dubious at best and that dosing the public water supply with a chemical amounts to mass medication.

And there is evidence to support both sides of the debate. So where do I sit?

If I listened to everything the doctors, obstetricians, and my fellow public health colleagues said I would have taken the epidural, stopped breastfeeding after 6 months and resisted our desires for co-sleeping. But I didn't. And it's usually when we're co-sleeping—with one child buried under the crook of my armpit, the other with a leg thrown across my belly where my intellectual wonderings as a public health researcher and natural parenting mama converge. And this is what I have discovered about fluoride and caring for our oral health.

So what is fluoride?

Fluoride ions (Calcium Fluoride CaF_2) are naturally occurring and come from the element fluorine, found in rocks, soil, plants, air and water. Proponents are quick to sell the 'natural' aspect of fluoridation, arguing that its addition to water is akin to fortifying or enriching foods such as adding zinc, iron or calcium to breakfast cereals, iodine to salt, or folic acid to flour. They say it's not adding a 'medicine', just tweaking the natural level of fluoride found in water. The problem with this argument is three fold. Firstly, the majority of what we see on food packaging is simply a distortion by the food marketers and manufacturers. Lollies laced with vitamin C or oven fries fortified with Omega 3 fatty acids with the promise of boosting brain functions of consumers are simply a distortion of science and examples of misleading nutritional value marketed as healthy food choices.

Secondly, fluoride, unlike calcium or magnesium, is not an essential nutrient for your body. If you were to consume zero fluoride your entire life, you wouldn't suffer for it. There's no such thing as fluoride deficiency.[87] And thirdly, while fluoride ions can be naturally occurring, these are not the ones added to drinking water and oral hygiene products. Queensland Health Water Fluoridation: Questions and Answers booklet states that the fluoride in our water are in fact sourced from scrubbers used in the manufacturing of fertilizers and that these scrubbers 'convert fluoride into a liquid or powder form (hydrofluorosilicic acid) that can be collected and safely added to water supplies'.

Despite reassurances from regulators that contaminant levels are 'extremely low' and conform to Australian Drinking Water Guidelines, fluoride sourced from scrubbers does not undergo purification procedures and has been found to contain various contaminants, including arsenic, lead and mercury. Along with fluoride, these contaminants bio-accumulate in our cells, bones, blood and organs, even in the pineal gland in our brains.

And overexposed to fluoride we are! Virtually all foodstuffs contain at least trace amounts of fluoride. When water is fluoridated, it is not just the water that is fluoridated, but all foods and beverages that are made with the water. As a general rule, the more processed a food is, the more fluoride it has. The highest dietary concentration of fluoride

---

[87] National Research Council of the National Academies, *Fluoride in Drinking Water: A Scientific Review of EPA's Standards*, Washington, DC: National Academies Press, 2006.

occurs in animal and processed foods, especially fish. Fluoride builds up in the tissues of animals, and whenever fluoridated water is used in food production, fluoride will be concentrated in the final product. The same goes for cooking with fluoridated water. And adults only excrete 50-60 per cent of the fluoride we ingest. Children only about 20 per cent and babies and the elderly, excrete even less. Fluoride even crosses the placenta in pregnancy.

BUT IT'S GOOD FOR OUR TEETH?

Fluoride is still the cornerstone of modern dental caries management. Fluoride acts as an enzyme inhibitor and is said to work by strengthening teeth, inhibiting demineralization, remineralising damaged enamel, and destroying the enzymes in the oral bacteria that produce the acids that erode the teeth. And there are some studies to support this. Researchers comparing topical and systemic fluoride action concluded that it was the topical application of fluoride in toothpaste and mouthwash products that is most beneficial.[88]

Even so, there are currently no labeling nor legal requirements to specify the type of fluoride being added to topical applications and there is currently no scientific evidence of a safe fluoride dosage per person given that fluoride consumption varies from person to person depending on their level of exposure.

Research also reveals that when fluoridation has been discontinued in communities from Canada, the former

---

[88] E Hellwig, & A Lennon, 'Systemic versus Topical Fluoride', *Caries Research*, 2004, 38: 258–262

East Germany, Cuba and Finland, dental decay has not increased but has generally continued to decrease.[89]

At a supermarket outing on a recent trip to the United States, we also noted that the US Food and Drug Administration (FDA) requires a poison warning on every tube of fluoride toothpaste sold in the US. The warning reads:

'If you accidentally swallow more than used for brushing, seek medical help or contact a poison control center immediately.'

Children swallowing too much fluoride toothpaste can suffer acute poisoning at doses as low as 0.1 to 0.3mg per kg of bodyweight. This generally presents in the form of gastric pain, nausea, vomiting, headache, dizziness, and flu-like symptoms. A child weighing 10kg needs only to ingest 1 to 3 grams of paste (less than 3 per cent of a tube of fluorinated toothpaste) to experience one or more of these symptoms.

The irony though, as my partner and I passed each other different brands of children's toothpaste, is that the manufacturers of children's toothpastes create products just beckoning to be eaten by children. They generally tend to be sweet, glossy, glittery, luminescent and smell of bubblegum, strawberries and sherbet. While I was examining the toothpastes, a mother leaned over my shoulder and told me she had recently taken to putting all the toothpaste in a safety cupboard out of her children's reach.

---

[89] L Seppa et al.. 'Caries trends 1992-98 in two low-fluoride Finnish towns formerly with and without fluoride', *Caries Research*, 2000,.34: 462-8; and G Maupome et al. 'Patterns of dental caries following the cessation of water fluoridation' *Community Dentistry and Oral Epidemiology*, 2001, 29:37-47.

Manufacturers in Australia are not legislated to put a warning label on our fluorinated toothpastes.

THE TOXICITY OF FLUORIDE

Fluorine compounds are listed by the US Agency for Toxic Substances and Disease Registry (ATSDR) as among the top 20 of 275 substances that pose the most significant threat to human health. The Australian National Pollutant Inventory (NPI) recently considered 400 substances for inclusion on the NPI reporting list. A risk ranking was given based on health and environmental hazard identification and human and environmental exposure to the substance. Some substances were grouped together at the same rank to give a total of 208 ranks. Fluoride compounds were ranked 27th out of the 208 ranks.[90]

HEALTH EFFECTS

The evidence of health effects are far reaching. A review of scientific literature by the Independent National Academy of Sciences found many gaps in the data about long-term health risks associated with exposure to systemically ingested fluoride. The authors found evidence of increases in dental fluorosis and called for more research on potential links with skeletal fluorosis, bone fractures, bone cancer, joint pain, thyroid damage, mental and physiological changes and dementia.[91] The National Research Council

---

[90] Government of Australia, *National Pollutant Inventory*, http://www.environment.gov.au/epg/npi/contextual_info/context/fluoride.html

[91] Dr. Paul Connett, '50 Reasons to Oppose Fluoridation', Accessed online at http://www.slweb.org/50reasons.html.

(2006), 'it is apparent that fluorides have the ability to interfere with the functions of the brain'.[92]

In 2012, Researchers at Harvard University published the results of a long-term analysis that links fluoridated water to lower IQ scores in children.[93] The researchers examined data on water fluoridation levels from a variety of medical databases and compared them to IQ scores of children who lived in the associated neighbourhoods. In total, 27 separate studies were examined which found a direct link between IQ scores and the levels of fluoride in the public water supply. Children in high-fluoride areas had significantly lower IQ scores than those who lived in low-fluoride areas. The children studied were up to 14 years of age, but the investigators speculate that any toxic effect on brain development may have happened earlier, and that the brain may not be fully capable of compensating for the toxicity.

'Fluoride seems to fit in with lead, mercury, and other poisons that cause chemical brain drain' says Phillipe Grandjean, adjunct professor of environmental health, Harvard School of Public Health. 'The effect of each toxicant may seem small, but the combined damage on a population scale can be serious, especially because the brain power of the next generation is crucial to all of us.'[94]

[92] 'Fluoride in Drinking Water: A Scientific Review of EPA's Standards', National Academy of Sciences, 2006.

[93] A Choi, G Sun, Y Zhang & P Grandjean, 'Developmental Fluoride Neurotoxicity: A Systematic Review and Meta- Analysis' *Environmental Health Perspectives*, 2012, October; 120(10): 1362–1368.

[94] See Harvard School of Public Health, 'Impact of fluoride on neurological development in children' http://www.hsph.harvard.edu/news/features/fluoride-childrens-health-grandjean-choi

How to reduce your daily exposure to fluoride and build resiliency

1. Stop drinking fluoridated water

Tap water consumption is the largest daily source of fluoride exposure for people who live in areas that add fluoride to the water. Avoiding consumption of fluoridated water is especially critical for babies and children. If you live in area which fluoridates its water (like 87 per cent of the communities in Australia) you can avoid drinking the fluoride in one of three ways:

Water Filters: Purchase a water filter. Not all water filters however remove fluoride. The three types of filters that can remove fluoride are reverse osmosis, deionizers (which use ion-exchange resins), and activated alumina. Each of these filters can remove over 95-100 per cent of the fluoride. By contrast, 'activated carbon' filters (e.g. Brita) do not remove fluoride. Harvesting and filtering rainwater is also an option and our preferred choice.

Spring Water: Purchase spring water. Most brands of spring water contain very low levels of fluoride. Some brands, however, contain high levels, so ask your supplier. Many suppliers also provide large reusable containers so you are not contributing to plastic consumption.

Water Distillation: A third way to avoid fluoride from the tap is to purchase a distillation unit. Water distillation will remove most, if not all, of the fluoride. The price for a distillation units varies widely depending on the size.

2. EAT A DIET OF WHOLE FOODS

A comparison of native and primitive societies have shown a high immunity to dental caries and freedom from degenerative processes compared with the diets of modernized groups who have forsaken their native diets for the foods of commerce—white flour products, sugar, polished rice, canned goods and vegetable fats.

Dental caries and gum disease are usually a sign of nutritional deficiencies and a toxic overload. Building resiliency means increasing nutrient dense foods in your diet. These include:

- Raw or cultured grass-fed dairy including, milk, cheese, cream, ghee, and butter;
- Clean sources of fat such as coconut oil, cod liver oil, butter and olive oil.
- Protein such as eggs and grass fed animal protein.
- Fermented or lacto-fermented condiments and beverages such as pickled vegetables, kefir and kombucha.
- Organically sourced vegetables and fruits.

3. BREAST FEED YOUR BABY

Fluoridated water, which contains up to 300 times more fluoride than breast milk, is by far the single largest source of fluoride for babies and infants. So without question, the single most important way to protect a baby from fluoride exposure is to breastfeed. Breast milk almost completely excludes fluoride and thus an exclusively breast-fed baby will receive virtually no fluoride exposure and will be provided with all the delicious and beneficial immuno-properties of breast milk.

If you're not breastfeeding, use clean, non-fluoridated water with organic cow or goat milk formula. (See 1)

4. SAY NO TO DENTAL FLUORIDE GEL TREATMENTS

Although dental researchers recommend that fluoride gel treatment should only be used for patients at highest risk of cavities, many dentists continue to apply fluoride gels irrespective of the patient's cavity risk. The fluoride gel procedure uses a concentrated acidic fluoride gel (12,300 ppm). Because of the fluoride gel's high acidity, the saliva glands produce a large amount of saliva during the treatment, which makes it extremely difficult (both for children and adults) to avoid swallowing the gel.

Even when dentists use precautionary suction devices, children and adults will still ingest some quantities of the paste, which can cause spikes of fluoride in the blood. The next time your dentist asks you whether you want a fluoride gel treatment, say no. Alternatively, seek out a holistic dentist who does not use nor recommend fluoride in their practice.

5. XYLITOL BENEFITS

Xylitol are sweet 'tooth-friendly' non-fermentable, sugar alcohols found in the fibers of many fruits and vegetables and can be extracted from various berries, corn husks, and birch trees. Unlike other sweeteners, xylitol has been found to be actively beneficial for dental health, including reducing dental caries[95] by inhibiting the Streptococcus bacteria that are significant contributors to tooth decay.[96] For dental use, you can find xylitol gums, toothpastes, lozenges, and rinses.

WHAT FLUORIDE-FREE BRANDS TO BUY?

Oral health impacts the whole body. When you have gum disease or plaque, inflammation of the whole body can occur. So getting your dental regime right is important. And there are some really good gums, pastes and rinses on the market. Our 'adult' favorites include: Ganozhi, Mukti Tooth Powder, and Oral Wellness. Our children love Spry Fluoride Free toothpaste or gel (with xylitol), gums and mints and Dr Tung's Floss.

MAKING A STAND

A boon for anti-fluorination campaigners came in November 2012 when the LNP Government passed legislation amendments to end government mandated water fluoridation in Queensland. If you would like more information, or to make a stand and get involved in the campaign contact the Queenslanders For Safe Water (www.qawf.org).

---

[95] P Milgrom P, K A Ly, et al., 'Mutans streptococci dose response to xylitol chewing gum' *Journal of Dental Research*, 2006, 85 (2): 177–181.

[96] A Maguire; A J Rugg-Gunn, 'Xylitol and caries prevention—is it a magic bullet?' *British Dental Journal*, 2003, 194 (8): 429–436. http://dx.doi.org/10.1038/sj.bdj.4810022

Plastics

Many changes that have occurred over the last hundred years have had such an incredible impact on the world that it's hard to image life before them. Plastic seems a small thing compared to electricity or cars or telephones, but it is everywhere. We store our food in it, sometimes eat with it, we give our kids toys made from it, we even make clothes and carpet with it. There's plastic in our computers, our cars, our everyday tools, even our furniture. Given how widespread our use of plastic is, particularly in food preparation and storage and children's toys, it is really important that we pay attention to the chemicals it brings into our homes, families, and bodies.

[19]

What Do the Numbers on Plastics Mean?

VANESSA LAYTON

*Vanessa Layton is an Australian mother of two who started Hello
Charlie when she moved back from the UK with her family and
discovered that many of the eco-friendly and baby-safe products she was
used to buying were just not available. Now they are. Find her at:*
http://www.hellocharlie.com.au

WHICH PLASTICS ARE healthier for you and more easily
recyclable? Do you know which plastics contain BPA?

The various plastic types are shown
by a number inside the triangular
recycling sign.

#1 PLASTICS: PET OR PETE
(POLYETHYLENE TEREPHTHALATE)

These are usually soft drink bottles, water or juice bottles. Easily recycled into products such as polarfleece, bottles and even carpet fibres.

PET can break down over time and leach, so it's best not to reuse these bottles. Recycle them straight away.

PET does not contain BPA, as it isn't used in the production of PET plastic.

Is it safe?

#2 PLASTICS: HDPE
(HIGH DENSITY POLYETHYLENE)

Used for milk bottles, juice and water bottles, as well as detergents, cleaners and skincare products. It's usually white or opaque.

HDPE can be recycled into all sorts of products, including pallets, other bottles, bins, pipes and even into park benches and children's playgrounds. It's also increasingly being used as recycled plastic toys.

HDPE is considered to be a safe plastic. It does not contain BPA.

#3 PLASTICS: PVC (POLYVINYL CHLORIDE OR PLASTICISED POLYVINYL CHLORIDE)

Used for things like plastic food wrap, plumbing pipes and cooking oil containers.

PVC can contain BPA and phthalates—it's best to avoid plastics with the #3 where possible. PVC plastics can also leach di (2-ethylhexyl) phthalate (DEHP), which is suspected of being a human carcinogen.

Is it safe?

#4 PLASTICS: LDPE (LOW DENSITY POLYETHYLENE)

Used for bread bags, supermarket bags and some food wraps.

Considered to be a safe plastic, but it's not very often accepted by recycling programs. Supermarkets will often have supermarket bag recycling bins in store.

Is it safe?

#5 PLASTICS: PP (POLYPROPYLENE)

Sometimes a cloudy plastic, like in sauce bottles. Sometimes it's clear, and sometimes it's coloured, like in yoghurt pots.

Does not contain BPA or phthalates, and is recommended for use as baby bottles, among other things. Easily recycled into things like worm farms and recycling bins.

Is it safe?

#6 PLASTICS: PS (POLYSTYRENE)

It's used in disposable plates and cups, as well as one use packaging, especially around electrical goods.

Polystyrene or styrofoam is another one to avoid, as it is not easily recycled and can leach styrene—a human carcinogen.

Is it safe?

#7 PLASTICS: OTHER (ALL OTHER PLASTICS, INCLUDING ACRYLIC AND NYLON)

This is a tricky one, as any plastic that doesn't fit into numbers 1 to 6 are lumped into #7 plastics—'other'.

As a general rule of thumb, it's best to avoid #7 clear plastics, especially polycarbonate (PC) as this contains BPA.

However, there are other plastics in this category that are BPA free and safe—these are the #7 opaque plastics.

ABS (Acrylonitrile Butadiene Styrene), which Lego is made from, is a safe plastic. BabyBjorn also use ABS—it's BPA free.

Plastics made from corn starch resin are lumped into the #7 category, and these are BPA free too.

Nylon is BPA free, and it's a #7.

The trick with this category is to avoid clear plastic #7, and to buy from a brand you trust (which means asking the manufacturer or supplier some hard questions!)

Is it safe? That depends on the plastic.

References

#7 plastics: http://www.boston.com/lifestyle/green/articles/2008/04/30/unlucky_number_7

More on #7 plastics:
http://www.nytimes.com/2008/04/22/health/22well.html?_r=1

Plastic Types: http://lifewithoutplastic.com/en/plastic-types

[20]

What is All the Fuss About BPA?

VANESSA LAYTON

Vanessa Layton is an Australian mother of two who started Hello Charlie when she moved back from the UK with her family, and discovered that many of the eco-friendly and baby-safe products she was used to buying were just not available. You can find her family tested list of products available, along with product reviews and cheat sheets at: http://www.hellocharlie.com.au

BISPHENOL-A (BPA) IS a chemical building block that is used to make polycarbonate plastics and epoxy resins. It's commonly used in clear, hard, shatterproof plastic containers, as well as in coatings on food and drink cans. BPA is used to make a whole range of products, from drink bottles and baby bottles, dental fillings and eyeglass lenses, to sports equipment and medical devices.

What's the problem with BPA?

It's an artificial oestroegen, and as such, is an endocrine disrupter. This means that in late pregnancy, for example, the hormones that are critical to brain development and the baby's development as a whole, can be messed about by these foreign chemicals.

BPA has been linked to a range of other medical issues, too, including chromosomal and reproductive system abnormalities, impaired brain and neurological functions, cancer, cardiovascular system damage, adult-onset diabetes, early puberty, obesity and resistance to chemotherapy.

What is being done about BPA?

Canada declared BPA to be a toxic substance in September 2010, and BPA is banned for use in baby bottles in the European Union, Denmark and the United Arab Emirates. Malaysia is due to ban BPA in baby bottles starting shortly, and China has also announced that it will no longer be using BPA in baby bottles, although there is no start date set for this yet. In the US, 10 states have imposed bans on the use of BPA in baby bottles and sippy cups.

Food Standards Australia New Zealand say they have no plans to ban BPA in Australia and New Zealand.

How do I avoid BPA?

Use alternatives to plastic, including glass, ceramic, silicone and stainless steel.

Avoid canned food and drink (that includes beer—switch to bottles!)

Know your plastics. Check the numbers and avoid plastic #3 (PVC) and clear plastics marked #7. Not all #7 plastics contain BPA, so check the packaging.

References

Wikipedia: http://en.wikipedia.org/wiki/Bisphenol_A
Environmental Working Group:
  http://www.ewg.org/chemindex/chemicals/bisphenolA
WA Today:
  http://www.watoday.com.au/wa-news/australia-wont-ban-toxic-bpa-20

[21]

Five Ways to Avoid Spreading and Absorbing BPA

Katy Farber is the author of Eat Non-Toxic: a manual for busy parents *and blogs at* Non-Toxic Kids, *a popular green parenting and environmental health blog which has been featured in* The Washington Post, Enviroblog, Terrain Magazine, *and others. Find her at* http://www.non-toxickids.net

YOU'VE UNDOUBTEDLY HEARD about BPA in water bottles, canned food, even in receipts. Now, a new study reveals that BPA is ending up in napkins, paper towels, toilet paper and business cards.[97]

---

[97] S. Neese 'Widespread BPA contamination in paper products, study suggests' *Envir. Health News*, January 2012, www.environmentalhealthnews.org /ehs/newscience/2011/11/2011-1205-bpa-paper-products

How? Thermal receipts are often recycled and then BPA ends up in new products with the recycled content. This chemical is everywhere! No wonder 93 per cent of Americans contain this endocrine disrupting substance.[98]

Here's how you can stop the spread of BPA from receipts.

1. Don't keep receipts in your reusable grocery bags, or you'll spread the chemical to your food, especially produce. I had been doing this for a while, and now realize that my receipts had been coming in direct contact with my organic, fresh vegetables.

2. In fact, refuse receipts when making purchases. Most of us do our banking online now, or you can use credit card statements to track your purchases. Or if you must get a receipt, place it in an envelope, where the BPA will not spread to other items.

3. Throw out receipts from your purse or wallet. Clean it out regularly. Wipe down credit cards and other contents to remove the chemical as much as possible.

4. And here is a great tip I found from Rodale:[99]
   Wash your hands—but avoid hand sanitizers. A recent Swiss study found that people who used those sanitizers then handled receipts absorbed more BPA into their skin than people who washed their hands before handling receipts.

---

[98] Alice Park 'Study Finds Spikes in BPA From Eating Canned Soup', *Time*, 11 November 2011, http://healthland.time.com/2011/11/23/study-finds-spikes-in-bpa-from-eating-canned-soup

[99] Emily Main 'BPA Found In Trace Amounts 'Everywhere'' *Rodale News*, 2011, http://www.rodale.com/bpa-in-paper?cm_mmc=Twitter-_-Rodale-_-Content-RodaleResearchFeed-_-keephomefreeofchemical

Yikes! A protective approach backfiring. That blasted hand sanitizer can have harmful chemicals (triclosan[100]) and increase BPA amounts.

5.   Wash your hands ESPECIALLY after handling money and before you eat, so you can avoid the transfer of BPA from your hands to your food.

And look how regulation can work, and reduce exposures:

'Ninety-four per cent of the thermal receipts – except those from Japan – had measurable levels of BPA. Undetectable levels in Japanese receipts are related to the 2001 BPA phase-out in that country. Measurable amounts were also found in receipts claiming to be 'BPA-free.''[101]

So, what are we waiting for? Banning BPA will have clear and measurable results, just like in Japan. Look at how successful removing leaded gas and lead paint have been. Let's get BPA out of our food, everyday items, and our bodies!

These dermal exposures are significantly less than food exposures, so be sure to reduce those exposures too.[102]

---

[100] See http://www.non-toxickids.net/search/label/tricolsan

[101] S Neese, 2012, op. cit.

[102] See Katy Farber, *Eat Non-Toxic: a manual for busy parents*, 2012. Details at http://www.non-toxickids.net/2011/10/eat-non-toxic-manual-for-busy-parents.html

Is BPS the New Mystery Chemical in BPA-free Plastic Food Containers and Cans?

ALICIA VOORHIES

Alicia Voorhies is a Registered Nurse and unapologetic medical research geek. She works with her mom and sisters to educate parents about the dangers of toxic chemicals in everyday products and their effect on growing children. The Soft Landing team specializes in childproofing and healthy home consultation for families.
http://guide.thesoftlanding.com

I'VE HEARD A LOT of panic about bisphenol-S (BPS) as a substitution for bisphenol-A (BPA) in sippy cups and water bottles, because as a new compound, little is known about its safety. A recent study indicates that even though it doesn't leach as easily, BPS is likely to cause problems similar to BPA by disrupting estrogen.[103]

I've been researching the prevalence of BPS in plastic food containers and canned foods for several months and here's what I've found so far:

- While there has been a documented substitution of BPS for BPA in thermal paper and dollar bills,[104] I haven't found any documented cases of BPS being substituted for BPA in plastic bottles and food storage. Folks seem to be drawing that conclusion from the study on BPS use in thermal papers.[105]

- There are a couple of newer BPA-free plastics I'm uncomfortable with because the ingredient lists remain undisclosed and not enough validated testing has been done to confirm the lack of estrogenic activity.

- As for BPS in canned foods: this is a greater possibility. We were super excited to hear that Campbell's is phasing out BPA in its metal can linings,[106] but the excitement

---

[103] René Viñas and Cheryl S Watson, 'Bisphenol S Disrupts Estradiol-Induced Nongenomic Signaling in a Rat Pituitary Cell Line: Effects on Cell Functions' *Environ Health Perspectives* 121:352–358 (2013). http://dx.doi.org/10.1289/ehp.1205826

[104] C Liao, F Liu, K Kannan, 'Bisphenol s, a new bisphenol analogue, in paper products and currency bills and its association with bisphenol a residues.' *Environ Science Technology* 2012 Jun 19;46(12):6515-22 http://www.ncbi.nlm.nih.gov/pubmed/22591511

[105] 'Widespread Exposure to BPA Substitute Is Occurring from Cash Register Receipts, Other Paper', *Science Daily*, http://www.sciencedaily.com/releases/2012/07/120711210241.htm

[106] The Soft Landing, 'Campbell's Responds to Concerned Parents and Commits to Removing BPA from Cans', 6 March 2012, http://guide.thesoftlanding.com/campbells-responds-to-concerned-parents-and-commits-to-removing-bpa-from-cans

wore off quickly when they refused to disclose what alternative lining will be used instead. And some of the possible alternatives like PVC and BPS are obviously worrisome.

How to Choose Safer Plastic Dishes and Food Containers

I've written about all of this in our free *Guide to Researching Safer Plastics* ebook,[107] but here's the basic gist:

1. Choose dishes and food containers made from plastics that never contained BPA in the first place, like polypropylene (PP), HDPE/LDPE, and silicone (talking about silicone dishes here, not bakeware[108]). They have a much better long-term track record than any other plastics and haven't been recently switched to BPA-free materials. Additionally, AS, SAN (used in Brita Water Pitchers), and ABS have a good track record for non-leaching stability so far too. Read more about that on my website.[109]

2. Only purchase canned and jarred food from companies who make it clear what their BPA-free lining is made

---

[107] Alicia Voorhies, *How to Choose Safer Plastics: Learn to do Your Own Research in Five Easy Steps*, 2011. Details at http://guide.thesoftlanding.com/learn-how-to-do-your-own-safer-plastic-research-with-our-free-guide/

[108] Alicia Voorhies, 'Is Silicone Safe for Kid's Dishes?' http://guide.thesoftlanding.com/newsletter/issue-2-is-silicone-safe-for-kids-dishes/

[109] The Soft Landing, 'What Type of Plastic is the BPA-free Baby Bullet Made From?' 2 February 2012, http://guide.thesoftlanding.com/what-type-of-plastic-is-the-bpa-free-baby-bullet-made-from

from. Bionaturae and its sister company, Jovial, are fantastic examples of companies with a conscience who use truly responsible food packaging.[110]

3. Don't even bother with products made by secretive manufacturers with mystery chemicals they refuse to disclose.

As my friend Beth of *My Plastic Free Life* points out, this process of trying to determine what chemicals a product already contains—and whether those chemicals are toxic—is COMPLETELY backwards![111]

The safest solution is to avoid newer plastics and stick with stainless steel or glass whenever you can.

In the meantime, I'll continue watching for new research and will keep you updated on my website!

P.S. Check out our Safer Food Storage Shopping Guide for plenty of great options.[112]

---

[110] See The Soft Landing, 'The Founder of Bionaturae Shares Her Insight on Making the Switch to BPA-free Canned Foods', http://guide.thesoftlanding.com/the-founder-of-bionaturae-shares-her-insight-on-making-the-switch-to-bpa-free-canned-foods

[111] Beth Terry 'Are BPA-Free Plastic Products, Food Cans, & Register Receipts Safer than Those with BPA in Them?' http://myplasticfreelife.com/2012/07/are-bpa-free-plastic-products-food-cans-register-receipts-safer-than-those-with-bpa-in-them

[112] The Soft Landing, 'BPA, PVC and Phthalate-free Food Storage Containers', http://guide.thesoftlanding.com/bpa-and-pvc-free-food-storage-containers

Cosmetics
& Skin Care

[23]

What Are the Main Chemicals to Avoid in Cosmetics?

KIRSTEN MCCULLOCH

Kirsten McCulloch is the editor of this book and an Australian writer passionate about living a more sustainable, healthy life—for herself, her family and the planet. She writes about non-toxic cleaning and other aspects of a healthy home at Sustainable Suburbia, where you can download her free Non-toxic Cleaning Printables.
http://SustainableSuburbia.net

'One third of all personal care products contain one or more ingredients classified as possible human carcinogens.'[113]

IF THAT STATISTIC isn't sobering enough, the US Environment Working Group also found in 2007 that 22 per cent of cosmetics and personal care products may be

---

[113] US Environmental Working Group, 2003, quoted in Sarah Lantz, *Chemical Free Kids*, 2nd Edition, 2012, p.106

contaminated with a cancer-causing impurity called 1,4-dioxane. You won't find dioxane listed as an ingredient, as it isn't added deliberately, but was revealed by cosmetic industry chemical safety assessments to be a contaminant in common petroleum-based cosmetic ingredients. Worse, those ingredients are found in 57 per cent of all baby soaps, and 34 per cent of all body lotions.[114]

It's not only carcinogens that we should be concerned about either. It's the hormone disruptors and allergens. It's the 45 per cent of products that contain at least one ingredient that could be harmful to your reproductive system or your baby's development. It's the 60 per cent of products that contain hormone disrupters and chemicals that mimic oestrogens. It's the 56 per cent of products that contain ingredients that help other chemicals penetrate your skin.[115]

In her book *Chemical Free Kids*, Dr Sarah Lanzt lists what she calls 'The Toxic Ten' in your beauty regime, ten of the most toxic chemicals in our daily cosmetics. She covers what the chemical does, the potential effects and where it's used.

Those chemicals are phthalates (see chapters 2 & 3 of this book), coal tar, formaldehyde, hydroquinone, lead acetate, nitrosamines (a contaminant often found in products

---

[114] 'EWG Research Shows 22 Per cent of All Cosmetics May Be Contaminated With Cancer-Causing Impurity',
http://www.ewg.org/news/news-releases/2007/02/08/ewg-research-shows-22-per cent-all-cosmetics-may-be-contaminated-cancer, viewed 10 October 2013.

[115] Lantz, op.cit. p. 107.

with DEA, MEW or TEA compounds), petroleum, phenylenediamine, alpha hydroxy acids and silica.[116]

Note that 'baby oil' is 100 per cent mineral oil, i.e. a petrochemical. If you want to give your baby a massage, steer clear of baby oil and stick to natural oils like almond and apricot kernel oils[117], or even just olive oil from your kitchen.

In the rest of this section you will find some details on specific chemicals and products as well as some recipes for how to make your own safer cosmetics, from deodorant to lip balm.

---

[116] ibid. pp. 111-116.

[117] Back when I was a professional massage therapist, a mix of almond and apricot kernel oils was my favourite blend to use.

[24]

What's in Our Products: A Brief Look at Parabens

Melissa Goodwin is a frugal mum of two, environmentalist, cook, crafter, bookworm and writer of the Australian blog Frugal and Thriving. *Connect with her on Facebook or find out why a frugal life leads to a thriving one on her blog.*
http://frugalandthriving.com.au/about/

ALMOST ALL PERSONAL care products, like your moisturiser and face cleanser, contain parabens. Parabens are petroleum based synthetic preservatives. They extend the shelf life of our products. Without preservatives, most of our skin care products and cosmetics would either have to be kept in the fridge or used within a few days.

It is the water content in products that make them susceptible to spoilage. Water makes an ideal environment for mould and bacterial growth, and when you open your skin care products, air borne spores come in contact with

155

the water and can potentially grow (this is why pure body butters[118] are easy to make and preserve—there is no water). Parabens have bactericidal and fungicidal properties that prevent bacterial growth, thus preserving personal care products and extending their shelf life.

When it comes to natural skin care alternatives, preservatives become an issue. As consumers, we expect our personal care products to have a long shelf life without refrigeration. But natural preservatives (such as grape seed extract) don't give the same results as parabens. Things in nature aren't meant to last forever. As a compromise, many natural products include parabens as their only synthetic ingredient.

The question is, are parabens safe or toxic? Mainstream cosmetic manufacturers and some studies argue that parabens are safe, that the amount used in cosmetics is relatively small, and studies that show parabens to be unsafe are argued to be inconclusive.[119]

On the other hand, the potential danger of parabens is that they mimic hormones, particularly oestrogen, and therefore upset the hormone balance in our body. A small imbalance in one hormone can result not only in an imbalance in other hormones, but also in other systems in the body

---

[118] See Melissa Goodwin, 'Make Your Own Natural Body Butter For Less' 23 October 2011, http://frugalandthriving.com.au/2009/make-your-own-natural-body-butter-for-less/

[119] M.G. Soni, S.L. Taylor, et al., 'Evaluation of the health aspects of methyl paraben: a review of the published literature', *Food and Chemical Toxicology*, Volume 40, Issue 10, October 2002, pp 1335-1373, http://www.sciencedirect.com/science/article/pii/S0278691502001072

(such as the nervous system). Hormonal imbalances, even minor ones, can affect our overall health.

Studies have revealed a link between high oestrogen levels and breast cancer and breast cancer tumours have been found to have parabens in them.[120] Exposure to parabens (along with BPA) is also thought to be a factor in early onset puberty.[121]

> 'Possible adverse effects of endocrine disrupters [such as parabens] include cancers, behavioural changes and reproductive abnormalities. The effects of endocrine disrupters are the greatest during foetal development and in juveniles. Effects on reproduction and the immune system have been reported for fish, alligators, seals and birds.'[122]

Other possible side effects of parabens include infertility in men,[123] allergic reactions and skin irritation.

---

[120] P.D. Darbre, A. Aljarrah et al., 'Concentrations of parabens in human breast tumours', *Journal of Applied Toxicology*, 2004, 24, pp 5–13. http://dx.doi.org/10.1002/jat.958

[121] See Elizabeth Weil 'Puberty Before Age 10: A New 'Normal'?' *New York Times*, 30 March 2012, http://www.nytimes.com/2012/04/01/magazine/puberty-before-age-10-a-new-normal.html?pagewanted=4&_r=0

[122] European Commission report 'Towards the establishment of a priority list of substances for further evaluation of their role in endocrine disruption:- preparation of a candidate list of substances as a basis for priority setting.' http://ec.europa.eu/environment/archives/docum/pdf/bkh_main.pdf

[123] Renata S Tavares et al. 'Parabens in male infertility—Is there a mitochondrial connection?' *Reproductive Toxicology*, Volume 27, Issue 1, January 2009, pp 1–7, http://dx.doi.org/10.1016/j.reprotox.2008.10.002

While parabens and many other chemicals used in our everyday products may prove to be safe after all, we have no strong evidence of their safety yet. Many of the current claims that parabens and other synthetic chemicals are safe are based on faulty logic.

Firstly, the statement that these chemicals are safe because they occur in our products in very small doses doesn't take into account that our exposure is compounded by using multiple products that include parabens. Parabens are in many, many products, including some food products. Because of this, we are getting anything but 'small doses'.

No study has ever assessed the long term effects of using these chemicals either alone or in relationship with the other synthetic chemicals in everyday products. While parabens may turn out to be safe, we don't know yet what a lifetime of constant exposure does to our health. Nor do we know the effect of one synthetic compound mixing with another (or multiple others) within the cells of our bodies once these chemicals are absorbed through the skin.

Finally, there is the often quoted logic of direct correlation. We assume that if there is no immediately discernible cause and effect, then there is no cause and effect at all.

This logic just does not do justice to the complexities of life and in this case, the human body. Just because a person doesn't immediately develop symptoms from using parabens, doesn't mean that disease developed later in life (or chronic illness earlier) was not in part caused by continual exposure to low doses of the synthetic chemical. Assuming that no immediate and direct correlation equals no correlation at all is short sighted.

There are many other common chemicals in our personal care products (actually there are over 10,000 synthetic chemicals in common use in personal care products, of which only about 11 per cent have ever been 'tested'). Some of these chemicals are known to be carcinogenic but are still used in cosmetics. However, sodium lauryl sulphate, petroleum and parabens are the top three most common synthetics. Avoid these and you can make a safe bet that you are avoiding the multitude of other chemicals.

[25]

Nanos and Sunscreen: Are Shade, Shirts and Hats the Safer Option?

KATE HENNESSY

Kate Hennessy writes about arts, health and wellbeing and travel. She is a music critic for the Sydney Morning Herald *and has written for* The Financial Review, Guardian Australia, Wellbeing Magazine, *and others. She teaches at the Australian Writers' Centre and helps brands like Channel 7, GetUp! and Sydney Theatre Company with written material. Find her at:*
http://www.katehennessy.com.au

AT 32-YEARS-OLD, the 'slip slop slap'[124] slogan is all grown up. Launched by the Cancer Council in 1981, it has reminded millions of Australians of the best ways to minimise skin damage from the sun.

---

[124] "Slip on a Shirt, Slop on Sunscreen and Slap on a Hat."

I've always practised the first instruction, 'slip on a shirt', probably because as a kid I was allergic to PABA (para aminobenzoic acid) so I learnt to protect my skin by covering up or risking an embarrassing rash. I still remember my mother's relief on discovering 'PABA free' sunscreen at the local chemist. Problem solved.

But while rashes are never fun, they pale in comparison to some of the potential risks of nano-materials in sunscreens today.

Remember the white-ish layer that sunscreen once left on your skin? This was the zinc oxide and titanium dioxide: the metals in the cream that protected your skin from the sun's rays. These days, the particle size of those metals is much smaller, meaning they rub on clear. No smeary white mask? The same protection? It's no wonder Australia's sunscreen regulator, the Therapeutic Goods Administration (TGA), says 'this has proved a popular option with consumers'.

But consumers may not know that because the particles are so tiny—thousands of times smaller than a strand of hair—there's a chance they may be absorbed into cells below the skin's surface, which they may damage.

Is there any evidence?

The TGA says there's no evidence nanoparticles can penetrate the skin, so no regulation is needed. European regulators are not so sure, however, and from July 2013 they will require the safety testing and labelling of nano-ingredients in sunscreens. From 2015, New Zealand will require the labelling of nano-ingredients in sunscreens and cosmetics.

'We are concerned the TGA is not current with science,' says Louise Sales, Nanotechnology Project Coordinator at Friends of the Earth (FoE), a long-term campaigner on the issue. 'An increasing number of studies suggest nanoparticles can penetrate the skin.'

If we accept for a moment they can penetrate our skin, what can they do? Louise points to a 2008 study that revealed certain nano-ingredients in sunscreen—anatase titanium dioxide to be precise—were breaking down the coating of Colorbond roofs.[125] 'This study really raised concerns about what it was doing to our skin,' says Louise.

In a previous Kidspot article, FoE's Dr Crocetti said there were fears nano-ingredients could lead to cancer and that 'people with damaged skin, young children and people who use sunscreens very regularly ... should avoid using nano-sunscreens.'[126]

BUT CAN'T YOU JUST AVOID USING THEM?

Avoid using nano-sunscreens. Sounds simple right? Well, no. Until recently, there were several brands readily available, including Invisible Zinc, Cancer Council and Woolworths

---

[125] Lisa Matthes 'Tests reveal potentially toxic titanium dioxide in sunscreen and cosmetics' http://www.foe.org/news/archives/2013-03-05-tests-reveal-potentially-toxic-titanium-dioxide-in-sunscreens-cosmetics

[126] Fiona Baker 'Sunscreen shock: Just how safe is sunscreen for our kids?' http://www.kidspot.com.au/familyhealth/Development-Sunscreen-shock-Just--how-safe-is-sunscreen-for-our-kids+7091+189+article.htm

Select, that claimed to be 'nanoparticle free'—a blessing for parents wishing to stay on the safe side. But a company called Antaria, which claimed to provide them with a 'nanoparticle' free product, supplied many of these brands. In December 2012, however, Antaria back-flipped, admitting its product was indeed a nano-material.

FoE is calling for Australia to follow suit with Europe by safety testing and labelling nano-ingredients in sunscreen. Meanwhile, we still want to spend time with our family outdoors, so if we can't trust the sunscreen labels, what can we do?

There are other sunscreens available with active ingredients known as 'molecular' UV absorbers. However, unlike the zinc oxide and titanium dioxide-based sunscreens, some don't offer broad-spectrum protection, meaning, they block UVB rays but not UVA rays.

'People using them may be exposed to high UVA levels which doesn't cause sunburn but can increase the rate of melanoma,' says Sales. In addition, while they do not contain nano-ingredients, they often do contain ingredients such as Octyl Methoxycinnamate and Oxybenzone. 'These are endocrine-disrupting chemicals which we would not recommend using either,' says Sales.

FIND THE OTHER OPTIONS

Australia has one of the world's highest rates of skin cancer and no one recommends discontinuing sunscreen use. But until parents can be assured sunscreens do not contain any potentially damaging ingredients, it may be back to zinc.

'Traditional zinc creams that rub on white are a good option,' says Louise.

It's also worth mentioning that in later years, 'seek shade or shelter' and 'slide on some sunnies' were added to the 'slip, slop, slap' campaign. Out of five possible precautions against the sun, just one involves sunscreen. Maybe I was a pretty enlightened kid, after all.

'Sunscreen shouldn't be our primary defence against the sun,' says Louise. 'Some call it chemical clothing and there's an element of truth to that.

'Covering up with real clothing is a great option. In countries in North Africa, for example, which are at similar latitude to Australia, they respect the sun, avoid the peak heat and wear protective clothing. Parents can also invest in very good bathing suits for kids that cover them up.'

EDITOR'S NOTE:

This article was first published on Kidspot.com.au in April 2013. Over 2012 and 2013 the FoE campaign for safety testing and labelling of nano-particles has attracted some criticism, largely based on the concern that people will avoid sunscreen altogether in order to avoid nano-particles.[127]

Much of the debate has hung on a government survey which asked questions about awareness of and perceived

---

[127] See for example Catherine Armitage, 'Sunscreen scaremongers given the slip, slop, slap', SMH, 1 April 2013. http://www.smh.com.au/national/health/sunscreen-scaremongers-given-the-slip-slop-slap-20130331-2h1l3.html

risk of using sunscreens with nanoparticles. However, the reporting on the survey has been largely based on two media releases dated February 2009, which stated that many respondents would 'rather risk skin cancer by going without sunscreen than use a product containing nanoparticles.' In fact, according to Swinburne University's research design expert Dr Vivienne Waller, this is a misinterpretation—if not a simple misrepresentation—of the survey's questions and answers. Firstly, the survey asked about risk perception, rather than behaviour, and secondly, a majority of respondents said they would avoid the sun altogether, or use long sleeves and hats, not that they would risk skin cancer.[128]

Other criticisms of the campaign rest on the fact that the research is still pending on nanoparticles, and that while there are studies showing that they may penetrate the skin and cause DNA damage, other studies suggest they do not. Therefore, the argument goes, we should not be suggesting people risk the known dangers of sun damage, to avoid the unknown dangers of nanoparticles. The European Union Scientific Committee on Consumer Safety (SCCS) Opinion, released in September 2012, is sometimes quoted,[129] which states 'on the basis of available evidence that

---

[128] See Katherine Wilson, 'The Nano-Suncreen Wars', *New Matilda*, September 2012, for more on this survey and the inaccurate media releases. https://newmatilda.com/2012/09/04/nano-suncreen-wars viewed 10 October 2013.

[129] See for example Paul Wright, 'Time to dispel the fear of nanoparticles in sunscreens', December 2012, http://theconversation.com/time-to-dispel-the-fear-of-nanoparticles-in-sunscreens-10856

the use of ZnO nanoparticles ... at a concentration up to 25 per cent as a UV-filter in sunscreens, can be considered not to pose a risk of adverse effects in humans after dermal application.' However, that same paper also acknowledges that zinc oxide *is* more toxic in the nano form. One study cited in the Opinion concludes that 'repetitive exposure to low concentrations of ZnO nanoparticles results in persistent or ongoing DNA damage.'[130]

In the end, the focus of the FoE campaign has never been to suggest that people avoid using sunscreen altogether. It is rather to effect a change in labelling laws, and insist on further safety testing.

Louise Sales again: 'If there is public concern about the safety of sunscreen, the fault lies with the TGA. If the TGA required labelling, consumers would have much greater peace of mind in knowing that what they are putting on their skin is safe.'[131]

FURTHER READING

For more information on the nasty chemicals in most commercial sunscreens, how to choose a safer option, or how to make your own, check out the links at: http://sustainablesuburbia.net/sunscreen/

---

[130] European Union Scientific Committee on Consumer Safety (SCCS) 'Opinion on Zinc Oxide (Nano Form)', September 2012, http://ec.europa.eu/health/scientific_committees/consumer_safety/docs/sccs_o_103.pdf.

[131] Catherine Armitage, 2013, op. cit.

[26]

Homemade Probiotic Deodorant That Really Works!

Andrea Muse is a Registered Nurse turned Frugally Sustainable Homemaker. She writes at Frugally Sustainable, *which she describes as the story of her family's 'transition out of a consumer culture into the brave world of sustainability.' She is the author of the ebook* Herbal Rescue: Your Guide to Creating a Homemade Herbal First Aid Kit. *Connect with her at:*
http://frugallysustainable.com/

PROBIOTICS. A buzzword within the natural health community. And rightfully so! Most health conscious individuals understand the positive effects on digestion that come from using probiotic foods and supplements. In fact, the benefits of ingesting probiotics have been well researched and the craze is taking over.

If you haven't already heard of fermented foods, kefir, and kombucha you will soon. These are nutritional powerhouses used by those seeking to live a healthy lifestyle through a superb digestive system. Courses such as the Lacto-Fermentation eCourse by Gnowfglins will give you the knowledge base you need in order to implement these cooking methods.

Likewise, as the known benefits of probiotics are now expanding into mainstream culture, new research is showing remarkable promise for the use of this 'good bacteria' in topical remedies.

Emerging thoughts include the idea that probiotics can actually help improve the balance of bacteria on your skin, very similar to the way they are known to improve the balance of bacteria in your digestive system. This will provide relief for those who suffer with eczema, psoriasis, various rashes of the skin, skin allergies, acne, unsightly discolorations, and interestingly enough it is also proving to be a powerful antidote against aging (a.k.a. wrinkles)!

Our skin is the largest organ in our body. It, above all, requires extreme care for overall health as it is our first line of defense against disease carrying pathogens. Often times we forget that our skin contains millions of beneficial bacteria, also known as micro flora. Micro flora provide an essential role in preventing undesirable bacteria from developing.

This is the part where we transition into what all of this means for our underarms (smile).

All of the chemicals in conventional deodorants serve to kill these 'bad' or undesirable bacteria that cause that unwanted natural scent. However, in the meantime, they kill the 'good bacteria' too. Leaving our bodies defenceless.

There are many reasons why we should be concerned about using anti-perspirants and commercially prepared deodorants! Here are just a few:

1. There are hidden dangers in the active ingredients of conventional deodorant[132] (i.e. aluminium, parabens, propylene glycol, phthalates, and triclosan). Current research shows a strong link between anti-perspirants containing aluminum and breast cancer, birth defects, allergies, and hormonal imbalances.[133] These potentially hazardous chemicals have no place in our homes and certainly no place under our arms.

2. Even with all of the options for an all-natural, 'green' deodorant,[134] it is simply too pricey for this frugal chick!

3. Let the body do what the body will do! I believe that when we attempt to inhibit the natural functions of the body we negatively effect the rhythms created for a purpose.

It was these concerns, and new research findings on probiotics, that lead me to create my own solution.

---

[132] Danna Norek 'Top five ingredients to avoid in deodorant' *Natural News*, August 2011, http://www.naturalnews.com/033364_deodorants_chemical_ingredients.html?Click=43799

[133] Sharyl Attkisson, 'Followup: Antiperspirants And Cancer' *CBC News*, 2006, http://www.cbsnews.com/stories/2009/06/29/cbsnews_investigates/main5123621.shtml

[134] Alexandra Zissu 'The 9 Best Natural Deodorants' *The Daily Green*, http://www.thedailygreen.com/environmental-news/latest/best-natural-deodorants-47062903

Homemade Probiotic Deodorant

Ingredients

- 1 tbsp. cocoa butter
- 1 tbsp. coconut oil
- 1 tbsp. shea butter
- 1 tbsp. beeswax
- 2 1/2 tbsp. arrowroot powder
- 1 tbsp. baking soda
- 1/4 tsp. vitamin E oil
- 15 drops essential oil of your choice
- 2 capsules powdered probiotics

Method

1. Melt cocoa butter, coconut oil, shea butter, and beeswax over low heat.

2. Remove pot from heat, then add arrowroot powder and baking soda. Whisk with chopsticks until all powders are dissolved and combined. Add vitamin E oil and essential oils at this time. Allow mixture to cool in pan. Once it is cooled and the consistency of pudding, open capsules of probiotics and add powder to mixture. Stir with spatula quickly to combine.

3. Add mixture to clean, used deodorant container. Place in refrigerator to cool and harden. After this, product may be stored on counter (Note: Using a shelf stable probiotic such as Bio-Kult will prevent the need for refrigeration). This recipe will fill container and last for 3-4 months. Remember...a little goes a long way!

NOTES

- When choosing a probiotic supplement for this deodorant it is important to find one that is shelf stable. It should also contain highly resistant beneficial bacteria such as lactobacillus and bifidobacteria. These 'good bacteria' have the ability to survive the pH of our stomach acid during digestion and are the ones that should be included in this recipe.
- If you have sensitive skin, omit the baking soda and increase the arrowroot powder accordingly. You may also consider omitting the essential oils.
- Use good smelling essential oils, any scent or combination of scents will do. So pick your favorite and have fun with it!

[27]

Forty Second Home Made Body Scrub

ALEXX STUART

Alexx Stuart is on a mission to help people eat better and be more conscious of what we use on our skin and in our homes, while eradicating guilt and feelings of deprivation. Her first book Real Treats *shot to #1 Amazon best seller within 12 hours of publishing. Alexx is also available for speaking engagements, workshops and commissioned articles.*
http://alexxstuart.com

I USED TO WORK in cosmetics. I worked for the most prestigious French skincare brand. Our body scrub was $122 retail and the top skin cream was a whopping $360 dollars—that was all the way back in 1997. I still remember the thrill of selling one as a counter girl, or later helping sell truck loads of them with my team of consultants once I was a senior manager. I genuinely believed I was doing good. I genuinely believed I was giving people the best they could afford. I genuinely believed the brand made our customers look and feel beautiful.

Turn back the clock however, and I'd have whispered in their ear (don't tell anyone, but just go get a jar of coconut oil, or a beautiful tube of Lavera or Cosima or Vanessa Megan and save yourself the money, the petrochemicals and the impending hormone related health problems).

I'm now 37 and honestly love the look of my natural skin. Now that the low fat, depleted nutrient days are over, my skin is plump, healthy and far from wrinkly. I still love my beauty products and have a few delicious natural ones in the cupboard, but I also am a big fan of the ol' DIY.

Here's a super simple scrub that will take you exactly 40 seconds to whip up, using spent coffee grounds, coconut oil, sea salt and vanilla extract. If you missed the video (my very first one. I'll get better, I promise!) it's on my Facebook page.[135] Gents, this is so easy, you could surprise your lady by making it for her as a pressie—not saying the boys shouldn't use this too. One for all and all for one!

HERE'S WHAT YOU NEED

- The spent ground coffee from an espresso
- 1 tablespoon of celtic / himalayan / fleur de sel sea salt
- 2-3 tablespoons of coconut oil (more oil = gentler scrub)
- 2 teaspoons of vanilla bean extract

WHAT TO DO

Mix in a bowl. Put into a jar. That's it. Takes less than a minute!

---

[135] See photos at https://www.facebook.com/Alexx.Stuart.Blog

[28]

Is Your Lip Balm Drying You Out? Here's How to Make Your Own

KIRSTEN MCCULLOCH

Kirsten McCulloch is the editor of this book and an Australian writer passionate about living a more sustainable, healthy life—for herself, her family and the planet. She writes about non-toxic cleaning and other aspects of a healthy home at Sustainable Suburbia, *where you can download her free Non-toxic Cleaning Printables.*
http://SustainableSuburbia.net

DO YOU USE a daily application of lipstick or lip balm, to moisturise and protect your lips? And okay, maybe for the aesthetic appeal too? Do you give lip balm to your kids to use too?

You do? Do you want the bad news first, or the good news?

The bad news: you might be surprised by just what you are smearing onto your skin, and just how 'moisturising' it actually is. Or isn't.

IS YOUR LIP BALM DRYING YOU OUT?

Commercially available lip products, including lip balm, frequently contain not only toxic chemicals (as if that were not quite bad enough), but chemicals that dry out your lips, making another application of said lip balm inevitable.

To avoid the drying out effect, skip products containing menthol, camphor, phenol or alcohol (OL).

DOES YOUR COLOUR CONTAIN HEAVY METALS?

There is more bad news about commercial lip products, especially lip stick. Studies in the US by the Campaign for Safe Cosmetics,[136] the FDA[137] and more recently by researchers at the University of California in Berkeley[138] have found unexpectedly high levels of lead and other heavy metals in many lipsticks. These won't be shown on any ingredients list, because they aren't deliberately added: they originate as contaminants, mostly in colouring agents. The

---

[136] See Campaign for Safe Cosmetics, 'Lead in Lipstick' http://www.safecosmetics.org/article.php?id=223 viewed 11 October 2013.

[137] FDA 'Lipstick and Lead: Questions and Answers' http://www.fda.gov/Cosmetics/ProductandIngredientSafety/ProductInformation/ucm137224.htm viewed 11 October 2013.

[138] Sa Liu, S. Katharine Hammond, and Ann Rojas-Cheatham 'Concentrations and Potential Health Risks of Metals in Lip Products' *Environmental Health Perspectives*, June 2013, 121:705–710; http://dx.doi.org/10.1289/ehp.1205518.

FDA says the levels are safe, and have not set an upper limit for contamination in the US.

Others disagree, citing the fact that no safe blood level of lead has been identified,[139] and no level of exposure appears to be safe for children.[140]

The European Union's Cosmetics Directive is sometimes cited as not allowing any level of lead, cadmium or chromium, however it is worth noting that while they do not allow them as ingredients, they do accept a certain level of contamination as inevitable.[141]

However, the Campaign for Safe Cosmetics notes that not all lipsticks tested contained lead—it is possible to produce lipstick commercially without it, by using different ingredients.[142]

---

[139] Centers for Disease Control and Prevention (CDC) 'Factsheet: Lead', updated July 2013, http://www.cdc.gov/biomonitoring/Lead _FactSheet.html, viewed 11 October 2013.

[140] David C Bellinger, 'Very low lead exposures and children's neuro-development' *Current Opinion in Pediatrics*: April 2008 - Volume 20 - Issue 2 - pp 172-177. See abstract at http://journals.lww.com/co-pediatrics/pages/articleviewer.aspx?year =2008&issue=04000&article=00013&type=abstract

[141] European Union, Joint Research Centre, 'Lead in lipsticks: safe levels of unintentional lead contamination confirmed' March 2013, http://irmm.jrc.ec.europa.eu/news/Pages/2603_lipstick.aspx, viewed 11 October 2013.

[142] Campaign for Safe Cosmetics, op. cit.

OR IS IT JUST PLAIN TOXIC?

In addition to the possible heavy metal contamination, some ingredients that can be found in commercial lip balm that you may want to avoid are:

* petroleum jelly or mineral oil
* paraffin
* parabens, including parahydroxybenzoate, butylparaben, methylparaben, propylparaben, and ethylparaben
* unspecified 'fragrance' or 'flavour'
* oxybenzone
* butylated hydroxytoluene (BHT)
* diazolidinyl urea
* octinoxate/ethylhexyl methoxycinnamate (this is a sunscreen ingredient)
* propylene glycol
* menthol, camphor, phenol and alcohol (which can all be drying)

The last piece of bad news: that is by no means an exhaustive list. If you have a particular product you are concerned about, you can check it out on the Environment Working Group's Skin Deep database.[143]

---

[143] You can use the EWG's skin deep database to search on products or ingredients. It ranks products and ingredients based on known dangers and (separately) on the level of research available. Note, though, that a product may receive a 'green' rating only because there is no research available, rather than because the research indicates safety. See http://www.ewg.org/skindeep/

But what's the good news?

There are two pieces of good news, in fact.

Firstly, you can check out Safe Cosmetic Australia's Toxic Free list, for products which only use ingredients allowed on their Permitted Chemicals list.[144]

Secondly, making your own lip balm is dead easy.

How to make your own luscious lip balm

The basic recipe for lip balm is 1 part liquid oil to 1 part beeswax, by weight. But you can be a bit more adventurous than that! Try this recipe for a choc-orange flavoured lip balm.

Ingredients:

- 10 g beeswax (about 3 tsp)
- 30g coconut oil (about 6 tsp)
- 14 g grated cocoa butter or shea butter (or use half and half) (about 3 tsp total)
- ½ tsp honey (approx. 4g)
- 1 tsp cocoa powder (approx. 3 g)
- 1/8 tsp or 12 drops natural vitamin E oil (about 2 capsules worth, depending on size)
- 3 drops sweet orange essential oil

Method:

Use a double boiler over a low heat. You can also use a low, wide mouth glass jar in a small pot of water. Just don't let any water accidently splash in, and keep the heat very low.

---

[144] See http://www.safecosmeticsaustralia.com.au

If you want to be precise and have an appropriate thermometer, heat the wax and oil to 68°C, and no more than 78°C.

Make sure you have lip balm containers ready, because the mixture starts to set almost as soon as you take it from the heat.

1. Place beeswax, coconut oil and cocoa or shea butter in the double boiler. Stir intermittently until it all melts. The beeswax will take longest. It's easiest to melt these together, because the beeswax on its own will resolidify the minute it hits your spoon. This step will take about 15-20 minutes.

2. Remove from heat, and whisk in honey, cocoa, vitamin E and essential oil. Keep whisking until the mixture is completely combined and smooth.

3. Transfer to lip balm tins or tubes and leave to set for at least three hours.

NOTES:

This recipe makes a little over ¼ cup. You can make less, but it's hard to get the measurements right unless you have jeweller's scales, and you'll lose a bigger proportion that sets in your saucepan or jar as you pour it out.

The honey is something of a preservative, and so is the vitamin E (which stabilises the oils). The cocoa and orange are just for flavour (and the cocoa adds a little colour too), though orange oil does have some microbial properties also. Just don't let your sweet-toothed child loose with this. You may find it all gets used up rather quickly. Trust me, I speak from experience.

ABOUT THE CONTRIBUTORS

Each chapter starts with an 'About the Author' section, so you do not need to be forever flipping back here to find out more about the qualifications and experience of the contributors. In most cases there is more detail here though. Many of them have other publications you can go to for more information, be it in print or ebook form, and all of them have websites. The only author bio I have left out of this section is my own, which you can find on the very back page of the book.

You can find more details of the contributors' stories on this book's website: http://lesstoxicliving.net.

NYREE BEKARIAN

Nyree Bekarian is a senior scientist at Exponent Inc and a contributing writer at Greenopedia.com. She has a Master's degree in Environmental Health Science and has previously worked for Environ International Corporation, the US EPA, and the Center for Children's Environmental Health at the University of California, Berkeley.
WEBSITE: http://greenopedia.com
TWITTER: http://twitter.com/nyree_1

NICOLE BIJLSMA

Nicole Bijlsma is a building biologist, author of the best seller *Healthy Home, Healthy Family* and CEO of the Australian College of Environmental Studies. She has featured on every major Australian television network and lectures and writes about the health hazards in the home. Her book is available from her website or good bookstores.
WEBSITE: http://www.buildingbiology.com.au

CATE BURTON

Cate Burton is a long term devotee of sustainable, chemical free living and to that end, set up Queen B Beeswax Candles over a decade ago. In her spare time she's a keen balcony veggie gardener and urban beekeeping enthusiast (with 2 beehives on her balcony) and runs Bees In The City.
WEBSITE: http://www.queenb.com.au
FACEBOOK https://www.facebook.com/QueenBcandles
TWITTER at http://twitter.com/queenbshive

JOANNA COZENS

Joanna Cozens is one half of the duo behind *Daily Organic*, a website dedicated to discovering, sharing and inspiring more Australians to live organically, sustainably, ethically; one step, one banana, one cleaning product at a time. Loving cooking good nutritious meals, living as frugally as possible, she's also a self-confessed wannabe *RocKwiz* diva who gets on her soapbox—regularly—about anything green.
WEBSITE: http://www.dailyorganic.com.au
FACEBOOK: https://www.facebook.com/DailyOrganic

SONIA DONALDSON

Natural New Age Mum is a little part of the internet where Aussie mum of two, Sonia Donaldson, shares her tips on living a happy, healthy, holistic lifestyle. The blog features topics on healthy whole food, living chemical free, saving the environment and inspiration for the soul.

WEBSITE: http://www.naturalnewagemum.com
FACEBOOK: http://www.facebook.com/naturalnewagemum

KATY FARBER

Katy Farber is the author of *Eat Non-Toxic: a manual for busy parents* and blogs at *Non-Toxic Kids*, a popular green parenting and environmental health blog which has been featured in *The Washington Post, Enviroblog, Terrain Magazine*, and others. Katy also writes for *Moms Clean Air Force, MomsRising*, and *Safer Chemicals*, and is the author of two books about education.

WEBSITE: http://www.non-toxickids.com
FACEBOOK: https://www.facebook.com/nontoxickids
TWITTER: http://twitter.com/Non_Toxic_Kids

TERAY GARCHITORENA KUNISHI

Dr. Teray Garchitorena Kunishi, ND is co-founder of the Berkeley Naturopathic Medical Group in Berkeley CA. Her workshops and programs provide solutions for depression, anxiety, fatigue, chronic stress, and insomnia, ADHD and PTSD.

WEBSITE: http://www.berkeleynaturopathic.com
FACEBOOK: https://www.facebook.com/BerkeleyNaturopathic

MELISSA GODWIN

Melissa Goodwin is a frugal mum of two, environmentalist, cook, crafter, bookworm and writer of the Australian blog *Frugal and Thriving*. She is also the author of the ebook *Plan Cook Save*, available from her website. Find out why a frugal life leads to a thriving one at her blog.

WEBSITE: http://frugalandthriving.com.au/about/
FACEBOOK: https://www.facebook.com/frugalandthriving

JO HEGERTY

Jo Hegerty is a journalist and copywriter passionate about inspiring small changes with big outcomes. She writes an eco-living blog for busy mums, and wrangles two kids, four chickens and a lively cattle dog in suburban Queensland. For tips and ideas on how to green your life, visit her website, *Down to Earth Mother*.

WEBSITE: http://www.downtoearthmother.com
FACEBOOK: https://www.facebook.com/DownToEarthMother

KATE HENNESSY

Kate Hennessy writes about arts, health and wellbeing and travel. She is a music critic for the *Sydney Morning Herald* and has written for News Limited papers, the *Financial Review* and *Guardian Australia*. She has reported from Peru and Turkey for *Wellbeing Magazine*, from the Solomon Islands for *Green Lifestyle*, from Germany for *Get Lost Adventure Travel* and from the NT for the *Guardian UK*. She teaches at the Australian Writers' Centre and helps brands like Channel 7,

GetUp! and Sydney Theatre Company with written material. Find her at:

WEBSITE: http://www.katehennessy.com.au
TWITTER: http://twitter@smallestroom.:

TRICIA HOGBIN

Tricia Hogbin in a project manager for The Australian Network for Plant Conservation. She is also an Australian writer and mother, who writes about learning to live better with less. She writes a regular column for the *Newcastle Herald* 'Less is More', as well as her blog, *Little Eco Footprints*.
WEBSITE: http://www.littleecofootprints.com

KATHARINE KOEPPEN

Katharine Koeppen, RA, LMT, NCTMB, is a US nationally registered aromatherapist, seasoned clinician, author and educator with twenty years in aromatic practice. An avid writer and blogger, her work has been published internationally by professional aromatherapy associations, magazines and peer-reviewed journals. Katharine is the owner of Aromaceuticals®, an essential oil company based in Dallas, Texas, and may be found online at:
WEBSITE: http://www.aromaceuticals.com
Aromaceuticals® is a registered trademark of Katharine Koeppen.

SARAH LANZT

Dr Sarah Lantz (PhD) is a researcher, writer and mother. She has a background in public and population health and specialises in the area of child and youth health and wellbe-

ing. Dr Lantz is the author of the bestselling book, *Chemical Free Kids: Raising Healthy Children in a Toxic World* and is currently a Research Fellow at the University of Queensland.
WEBSITES: http://www.chemicalfreekids.com.au
http://www.nontoxsoapbox.com

VANESSA LAYTON

Vanessa Layton is an Australian mother of two who started *Hello Charlie* when she moved back from the UK with her family, and discovered that many of the eco-friendly and baby-safe products she was used to buying were just not available. You can find her family tested list of products available, along with product reviews and cheat sheets about baby products and particular chemicals on her website:
WEBSITE: http://www.hellocharlie.com.au
FACEBOOK: https://www.facebook.com/hellocharlie.com.au

ANDREA MUSE

Andrea Muse is a Registered Nurse turned Frugally Sustainable Homemaker. She writes at *Frugally Sustainable*, which she describes as the story of her family's 'transition out of a consumer culture into the brave world of sustainability'. You can download her free ebook *Herbal Rescue: Your Guide to Creating a Homemade Herbal First Aid Kit*, from her website.
WEBSITE: http://frugallysustainable.com
FACEBOOK: https://www.facebook.com/frugallysustainable

ALEXX STUART

Alexx Stuart is on a mission to help people eat better and be more conscious of what we use on our skin and in our homes, while eradicating guilt and feelings of deprivation. Her first book *Real* Treats shot to #1 on the Amazon best seller lists within 24 hours of publication. Alexx is also available for speaking engagements, workshops and commissioned articles.

WESBITE: http://alexxstuart.com

FACEBOOK: https://www.facebook.com/Alexx.Stuart.Blog

ALICIA VOORHIES

Alicia Voorhies is a Registered Nurse and unapologetic medical research geek. She works with her mom and sisters to educate parents about the dangers of toxic chemicals in everyday products and their effect on growing children. The Soft Landing team specializes in childproofing and healthy home consultation for families who are interested in protecting their loved ones from physical harm and from toxic chemical exposure.

WEBSITE: http://guide.thesoftlanding.com

FACEBOOK: https://www.facebook.com/thesoftlanding

SARAH WILSON

Sarah Wilson is a journalist and TV presenter who writes about 'how to make life better'. She describes herself as on a mission to find ways to make life bigger, more meaningful, nicer, smarter, healthier. Sarah is the author of the recently released best-seller *I Quit Sugar*, as well as the best-selling ebooks: *I Quit Sugar: an 8-week program* and *I Quit Sugar Cookbook*.

WEBSITE: http://www.sarahwilson.com.au

Special Bonus Downloads

This book contains lots of great information to get you started on your journey to a less toxic life.

To help you get going, we've created a goodie bag of extra material for you, including printables and additional special content.

Just open your web browser and go to

Lesstoxicliving.net/free-bonus

Fill in the form including the access code: **PB-BONUS**

Then check your in box for an email from me, Kirsten@SustainableSuburbia.net, and click on the link to go to your special bonus download page.

Enjoy!

Index

ABOUT THE AUTHOR

Kirsten McCulloch is an Australian writer and mother,
passionate about living a more sustainable and healthy
life— for herself, her family and the planet. She writes
about sustainable living, non-toxic cleaning, health, and
parenting. She has a Master's Degree in Writing and
Literature, and a long history of working with
environmental and natural health organisations, from her
time volunteering for The Wilderness Society to working as
a qualified massage therapist and teacher. From there it
was a natural step after becoming a mother, to start
considering how our consumer practices and
environmental toxins are affecting not only the
environment, but our children as well. She has written for
various online and offline publications. Find her at
SustainableSuburbia.net or on twitter @sustainsuburb.

12723647R00120

Printed in Germany
by Amazon Distribution
GmbH, Leipzig